MW01193519

CEO Guide to Doing Business in Mexico

By Ade Asefeso MCIPS MBA

Second Edition

ISBN-13: 978-1499542820

ISBN-10: 1499542828

Publisher: AA Global Sourcing Ltd
Website: http://www.aaglobalsourcing.com

Table of Contents

Disclaimer

This publication is designed to provide competent and reliable information regarding the subject matter covered. However, it is sold with the understanding that the author and publisher are not engaged in rendering professional advice. The authors and publishers specifically disclaim any liability that is incurred from the use or application of contents of this book.

If you purchased this book without a cover you should be aware that this book may have been stolen property and reported as "unsold and destroyed" to the publisher. In this case neither the author nor the publisher has received any payment for this "stripped book."

Dedication

This book is dedicated to the hundreds of thousands of incredible souls in the world who have weathered through the up and down of recent recession.

To my family and friends who seems to have been sent here to teach me something about who I am supposed to be. They have nurtured me, challenged me, and even opposed me…. But at every juncture has taught me!

This book is dedicated to my lovely boys, Thomas, Michael and Karl. Teaching them to manage their finance will give them the lives they deserve. They have taught me more about life, presence, and energy management than anything I have done in my life.

Introduction

This book is aimed at companies experienced in overseas trade which are new to doing business with Mexico. You may be an exporter looking to sell directly to Mexican customers or through an agent or distributor in that country. Alternatively, you may be planning to set up a representative office, joint venture or other form of permanent presence in Mexico.

This book aims to provide a route map of the way ahead, together with signposts to sources of help.

It identifies the main issues associated with initial research, market entry, risk management, and cultural and language issues. It also includes questions you should ask at the beginning of your research into Mexico.

I do not pretend to provide all the answers in this book; but it will point you in the direction of the people, organisations and publications that will be able to answer these and other more detailed questions.

The objective of this book is to steer companies through the initial research and preparation stages of entering the Mexican market. It is far better to spend time and money carrying out thorough research and preparation before entering the market than to enter Mexico in a rush, only to discover, when it is too late, that you have made a poor and expensive decision.

Doing Business in Mexico

Following three centuries under Spanish rule, Mexico finally achieved independence early in the nineteenth century. The subsequent period in Mexico's history was dominated by civil war, European intervention, a long domestic dictatorship and perhaps the most important event in the twentieth century, the Mexican Revolution. This influenced Mexican culture and politics for more than half century as Mexico's could have been easily described as one-party political system, until elections held in July 2000 saw a defeat for the Institutional Revolutionary Party.

Today Mexico's political landscape is a thriving democracy with three political parties, competing neck and neck to govern the country. Despite the economic crisis of the mid-nineties, Mexico's economic achievements are many. The country's increasing manufacturing output, rich natural resources and major exports have resulted in a significant recovery in the economy, which continues to improve well into the twenty-first century and invites foreign business from across the globe. Mexico's economy largely shadows the economic cycles of it powerful neighbour the USA.

Mexico is a country of huge potential which has demonstrated predictable, stable economic growth. It is a dynamic market and analysts predict that its economy will be the world's seventh largest by 2050.

It covers an area about the same size as the whole of Western Europe and occupies a strategic global position, being the natural bridge between Latin America to the south and the United States and Canada to the north.

Mexico is the largest trading nation in Latin America and one of the world's top 15. As the economy has grown so has the demand for imports. UK exports of sophisticated goods and services have grown due to that demand.

Mexico was the first Latin American country to become a member of the Organisation for Economic Co-operation and Development (OECD) and is also a founding member of the World Trade Organization (WTO).

Mexico has free trade agreements with more countries than any other in the world – 12 agreements with 44 countries. Mexico is expected to continue expanding its network of agreements to diversify its export markets and to attract foreign enterprises to invest and reap the benefits of joint production in a strategic location.

Chapter 1: EU–Mexico Free Trade Agreement

The EU–Mexico Free Trade Agreement has led to the elimination of all tariffs on EU-origin industrial goods. With no import duties, UK exporters can now compete on equal terms with exporters from the USA and Canada who also enjoy preferential access to the Mexican market. The agreement came into effect in July 2000 and is one of the most comprehensive foreign policy instruments ever signed by Mexico. It is known as the "Global Agreement" and has three main streams: political dialogue, co-operation, and commercial liberalisation.

The liberalisation programme for Mexican products was concluded on 1 January 2003, while the one for European products being exported to Mexico was concluded on 1 January 2007. The Global Agreement also promotes the agricultural sectors and establishes a legal framework for the liberalisation of trade in services, foreign direct investment promotion, protection of intellectual property rights, government purchases and the resolution of disputes.

Mexico – a gateway to the USA (NAFTA)

Although there is no EU free trade agreement with the USA, British companies can take advantage of Mexico's Free Trade Agreement with the USA and Canada (North American Free Trade Agreement, or NAFTA). By establishing themselves in Mexico, British companies can use Mexico as a low-cost manufacturing base with direct, duty-free access to the largest consumer market in the world, the United States.

Signature of free trade agreements
1994 – Mexico–USA and Canada (NAFTA)
1995 – G3 between Mexico, Venezuela and Colombia (Venezuela has since withdrawn from the treaty)
1995 – Mexico–Costa Rica
1995 – Mexico–Bolivia
1998 – Mexico–Nicaragua
1999 – Mexico–Chile
2000 – Mexico–Israel
2000 – Mexico–European Union
2001 – Mexico–Norway, Switzerland, Iceland and Liechtenstein
2001 – Mexico–El Salvador, Guatemala and Honduras
2004 – Mexico–Uruguay Economic Partnership Agreement
2005 – Mexico–Japan

Chapter 2: Why Mexico?

Mexico's economy is the world's eleventh largest: larger than Canada's and Australia's, and just behind Italy's (World Bank´s gross domestic product (GDP) ranking, purchasing power parity (PPP) based).

At the beginning of 2011, the real economy (indicators related to production) was continuing to perform reasonably well, buoyed by robust internal demand. Due to the existence of a competent, independent central bank, inflation is both low and stable while interest rates are at a historically low level. Foreign direct investment into Mexico has been booming in recent years (US$19.8 billion in 2010), due to solid macroeconomic fundamentals and the benefits of NAFTA.

Many large original equipment manufacturers (OEMs) are choosing Mexico as a base, which has created significant supply chain opportunities for smaller companies, particularly in the industrial zones located near the USA. This, complemented by a well-educated workforce, has meant that Mexico is now moving up the value chain – away from the traditional maquiladoras (assembly plants) and textile industries into engineering, IT, research and development, and the creative industries. In recent years the maquiladoras have focused on more sophisticated manufacturing operations, in line with the modernisation of the Mexican economy.

Economic situation

As with any new market, it is essential to research and plan your strategy for Mexico. Mexico is a very competitive market and it is important to take a medium- to long-term view. Doing business in Mexico can seem daunting for those new to the market, but taking a strategic approach is the key to making the process manageable.

If, after your initial background research, Mexico is part of your strategic plan for overseas development, then you are ready to start the next phase: market research. In many sectors, Mexico is already a well-developed market. You may find that your competitors are already there and that competition is fierce.

As in any new market you will need to use your competitive advantages to the full, and it is important to know which ones will be the most effective in Mexico.

You will need to research the market to identify the level of demand for your product and to decide whether you should address the market as a whole or via specific niches.

When considering Mexico as an export market, the following points are important:
- Leave your preconceptions at home.
- Keep hold of your business sense as tightly as you would anywhere else.

- Do your homework on the market and on potential partners.
- Be patient, as some things may take longer to set up than you think (especially if they involve bureaucracy). Allow for this in your preparations.
- Take a long-term approach, but don't stick rigidly to your plans. Things often change rapidly and unexpectedly in Mexico.
- Obtain good quality independent legal and professional advice, particularly concerning intellectual property.
- Do your research on local business culture.

Once you have confirmed that there is a market for your product in Mexico you may want to use the information you have gathered as a basis for developing a formal Mexico strategy. This strategy should address questions such as the form of market entry (setting up a subsidiary, distributor or agency agreement, or joint venture), identification of customers, potential partners, geographical locations, sales structure, product delivery and payment channels, and after-sales setup.

Mexico is a very competitive market and it is important to take a medium- to long-term view.

Chapter 3: Opportunities in Mexico

Mexico is a country full of opportunity and there has never been a better time to consider Mexico as a place to do business. British perceptions of Mexico are frequently inaccurate. Mexico is a modern, dynamic place in which to do business. The Mexican Government and businesses are committed to reducing their dependency on trade with the USA. With its impressive network of Free Trade Agreements (including North America and the EU) and its strategic location between the USA and Latin America, Mexico has the potential to act as a springboard into the region as well as being an attractive market in its own right.

The past decade has seen sound management of public finances, with prolonged economic growth and stable inflation. Mexico regularly ranks in the top three emerging markets in which to do business and is a country ready and open for business. The UK exports less to Mexico than many of our major competitors. So, while the opportunity clearly exists, others are taking greater advantage of it.

Mexico currently has free trade agreements with 44 countries in three continents, more than almost any other country in the world. Mexico is expected to continue expanding its network of agreements to diversify its export markets and to attract Mexican and foreign enterprises to invest and reap the benefits of joint production in a strategic location.

EU-Mexico Free Trade Agreement

The EU-Mexico Free Trade Agreement allows British industrial goods and other qualifying exports to enter Mexico, tariff free. This agreement also guarantees access to public tender offers in Mexico for EU companies.

North American Free Trade Agreement (NAFTA)

NAFTA is the free trade agreement between Canada, Mexico and the United States of America.

Since the advent of the EU-Mexico free trade agreement, British manufacturers have been able to export industrial goods to Mexico on equal terms to those enjoyed by American and Canadian exporters, as they do not pay Mexican import duties. NAFTA may also present advantages for British companies, particularly in the absence of a free trade agreement between the EU and the United States. By establishing themselves in Mexico, British companies can use Mexico as a low-cost manufacturing base with direct, duty-free access to the largest consumer market in the world, the United States.

NAFTA has led to the creation of numerous manufacturing operations based in Mexico that are able to supply the USA and Canadian markets. Excellent export opportunities exist for British tier two and tier three manufacturers who already supply similar operations in Europe to supply these operations in Mexico.

With a population of 112 million people, including a large and growing middle class, Mexico is a significant potential consumer market. It is the UK's second largest export market in Latin America after Brazil and it is the number one receptor of Foreign Direct Investment in Latin America. In fact, the UK is one of the largest investors in Mexico and demand for UK goods and services extends across the economy from sectors as diverse as education and infrastructure to food and drink.

The Mexican Government is actively working to reduce bureaucracy and improve competitiveness, and is driving forward reforms to attract new investment and diversify trade and many of the potential pitfalls can be avoided with adequate preparation.

UK Trade & Investment helps companies of all sizes do business in Mexico through a network of international trade teams based in the English regions and devolved administrations. In Mexico, there are dedicated trade & investment teams based in Mexico City, Monterrey, Guadalajara, and Tijuana.

Mexico is the largest military and commercial aircraft market in Latin America. It has the second largest business aircraft fleet in the world and has a large private aviation services industry to service the oil and gas sector and provide executive transport. Mexico is striving to develop the capacity to assemble executive jets in the next 6-8 years. Mexican aerospace imports are spread evenly between aircraft and aircraft parts, aero-engines and avionics. After China, Mexico is forecast to be the second largest market for the Aerospace sector in the next two decades.

The Mexican Government has targeted aerospace as a strategic industry in its economic development strategy. Government, industry and academia are co-ordinated in their approach to attract foreign investment.

There are around 240 aerospace manufacturing companies employing over 30,000 individuals. The main clusters are located in the north and the Northern States and Central State of Queretaro. In recent years the sector has attracted significant investments from some of the largest companies in the sector including Honeywell, Bombardier, Bell, Cesna, GKN, Meggitt and Triumph.

Chapter 4: Aerospace and Automotive Opportunities

Trac Precision Machining, part of the Trac Group Ltd, started manufacturing its turbine blades for commercial jet engines and power generation equipment in Mexico in 2009.

The company has signed an agreement with The Offshore Group, which has enabled companies to establish and maintain manufacturing facilities in Mexico at low cost and risk since 1986.

Trac Group's decision to locate manufacturing in Mexico was based on its need to grow capacity to meet customer needs; lower its base cost for manufacturing; and to meet demand by customers to source in U.S. currency. One of its biggest customers is Rolls Royce, with whom it will share 50 percent of the capacity of the Sonora operation.

Mexico exported over US$3.2 billion in aerospace manufactures and services in 2010. This figure is expected to exceed US$5 billion by the beginning of 2013.

Mexico is the ninth largest automotive producer in the world, currently producing just over two million vehicles annually. Mexico has also become the auto parts hub for North America. The Automotive sector in Mexico has attracted some of the largest Original Equipment Manufacturers (OEMs) mainly from the

USA and Japan and provides excellent opportunities for supply chains from tier one to tier four suppliers (domestic and foreign). Mexico is also the home to 13 heavy cargo vehicle OEMs.

In the past decade, Asian and European auto-parts suppliers have invested heavily in the USA and now analysts predict a wave of new investment in Mexico. Major investments by the main automakers and new free-trade activity are triggering further expansion as well as a move to more advanced and lighter weight vehicles and those with fewer emissions. Automobile suppliers now see Mexico as a viable production centre for all of North America.

UKTI's office in Monterrey has good relations with the main automotive clusters including government offices such as ProMexico, the Mexican organisation responsible for foreign trade and direct foreign investment and the main automotive trade associations.

Mexico is the ninth largest automotive manufacturer and the sixth-largest auto exporter in the world. It is the most important manufacturing platform for the Americas.

GKN Driveline has grown continuously since it started production of CVJ Systems in Mexico in 1979.

A state-of-the-art technology centre opened in 1997. In addition a precision forge was established in 2000, producing a wide variety of extrusions. To support the growing market for CVJ Systems in Mexico and the USA an assembly facility opened in 2006 at Villagran.

Chapter 5: Consumer Goods Opportunities

Since early 2008, a number of high-end UK designer labels have established themselves in Mexico. Burberry, Hackett and Thomas Pink now have in-store boutiques in Palacio de Hierro, Mexico's high-end department store.

In addition to this, several brands are expanding their network of free standing shops around the country.

In May 2010, Accessorize opened their first shop in Mexico City which surpassed all expectations and drove the managers to open their second shop. Two additional shops opened in 2011 and the company is now considering expansion in the main Mexican cities. UK brands are considered high-end in Mexico.

The consumer goods sector in Mexico has grown rapidly over the last five years and prior to the current global economic downturn, increasing affluence, access to credit, a growing population; including a larger number of young people and the continuing development of organised retail infrastructure are key factors behind the forecasted growth in Mexico's retail sales. Sub-sectors include: Fashion, cosmetics, shoes, jewellery, toys and furniture.

Luxury Goods

UK designer brands are in high demand particularly by department stores. Burberry has been in the market for over 5 years and is now expanding its presence across main cities in Mexico.

Cosmetics

Mexico is one of the leading markets for cosmetics in Latin America, the industry is valued at approximately US$8,000 Million and there are over 200 companies in the cosmetics and toiletries sector.

Jewellery

British jewellery retailers have already penetrated the market: Accessorize launched four stores between 2010 and 2011 in Mexico City.

Footwear

Mexico is recognised internationally for its excellence in the manufacture of footwear. Both the states of Guanajuato and Jalisco stand out in this area, since they have an experienced work force and have focused their efforts on targeting this niche area. There are more than 800 companies in this sector.

Mexico is one of the largest luxury goods market in Latin America and international brands tend to experience rapid growth after entering the Mexican market.

Chapter 6: Creative Industries Opportunities

Creative and Media is a growing sector in Mexico and it accounted for 7 per cent of GDP in 2010. During that year, Mexico exported creative goods and services to the value of aprox US$5 million and is ranked number one in terms of creative economies in Latin America and top 20 worldwide. The growth of the sector has created a large number of jobs and made it the fourth most important sector in the Mexican economy. Subsectors include TV, broadcasting, film, publishing, music and fashion where 11 per cent of Mexican jobs are related to these industries.

In terms of entertainment, Mexico now features on the tour schedule of most mainstream British bands and is beginning to feature more on the schedule of up and coming bands.

The cinema market is huge in Mexico; in fact it's the largest cinema market in Latin America.

Mexico will increase investment in the internet publishing sector. By 2013, 2.2 per cent of the overall private investment in the publishing sector will be targeted to the internet.

In 2011, BBC Worldwide launched its new HD channel after three years in Mexico. Their two other branded channels have been increasingly popular among the Mexican audience and shows such as Top Gear are now very popular in Mexico.

Mexican media are generally quite receptive to British brands therefore it is easier to secure press coverage for several UK companies.

Creative and Mediaas the Digital Creative City.

The project includes the construction of the first cluster in Mexico focusing in attracting technology companies devoted in developing; videogames, movies, multimedia and mobile applications.

Guadalajara is becoming the most important place to be for digital media production companies and has been designated by the Federal Government.

Chapter 7: Education and Training Opportunities

Education and Training is a high priority for the Mexican Government. According to the latest Organisation for Economic Co-operation and Development (OECD) reports; the government expends 22 per cent of total public funds to education, around 7 per cent of the GDP. In the Government's plans, education in Mexico will concentrate on five pillars: upgrading of the education infrastructure; continuing to incorporate Information and Communications Technology (ICT) in classrooms; vocational training and permanent evaluation and educational reform. The Federal Education Ministry is committed to reducing the urban-rural gap by investment and technological training.

A new educational reform has come into force, and a National IT Skills Programme was introduced. The Programme aims to create a major change in traditional educational models of primary and lower secondary, virtual lower secondary and the educational programmes for the indigenous groups, by applying ICT teaching models.

Through the educational reform and the IT Skills Programme, the Ministry of Education has approved a US$40 million budget, aiming to equip 350,000 classrooms and 700 ICT programmes for teachers by 2012.

Higher education enrolment has seen a strong and steady increase since 2000. Private sector enrols about 33.5 per cent and public universities do not have the capacity to cover the total demand, creating a market for private institutions. Private institutions have increased their fees and students able to afford the cost of private institutions are a serious target audience for UK education providers.

In 2010-2011, more than 34.4 million students finalised studies from basic to higher education levels, accounting for the 28.6 per cent of the Mexican population; with a faculty of 1.8 million teachers in 249,700 schools.

Chapter 8: Environmental Opportunities

With the development of environmental legislation and increasing awareness in the country, Mexico's environmental market has been rapidly and steadily growing at an annual average of 6 per cent since 2004.

According to the Mexican National Institute of Ecology, it is the second most important environmental market in Latin America after Brazil and is estimated to be worth approximately US$8 billion in total.

Demographic and industrial growth has placed extreme pressure on Mexico's ecological systems. These trends have caused the deterioration of air, water and soil quality in most regions of the country. In fact, the lack of clean water and deforestation are actually considered national security issues by the Mexican Government and air pollution, particularly in Mexico City, has long been a public health problem.

Mexico imports a high share of its environmental equipment and services to meet the growing demand, which is generating an increasing pool of good opportunities for UK companies. For environmental technology exporters, a federal tax incentive programme has been introduced allowing private companies to write off the value added tax for the purchase of pollution control equipment used to comply with environmental regulations.

Climate change is a priority for the Mexican government, which has made it a cornerstone of its 2007-2012 National Development Plan (the basis for all of the policies of the current administration). Mexico is one of the first developing countries to commit to a voluntary carbon reduction target to combat climate change. The goal is to reduce 51 million tonnes of CO_2 by 2012; however, according to the Mexican Ministry of Environment and Natural Resources, by 2010 the country had already reduced 21 million, which represents more than 40 per cent of the total.

Because of the high carbon intensity of its energy supply, there is still considerable scope for reducing greenhouse gas emissions in the operating segments of the state-run oil company PEMEX and the national power supplier CFE.

Business Opportunities
- Waste management and recycling
- Water pollution control
- Air pollution control
- Contaminated land remediation
- Environmental monitoring equipment
- Consultancy
- Energy efficiency
- Green house gas capture and storage
- Carbon trading

Mexico is the fourth most active country in the Clean Development Mechanism scheme (CDM), accounting for 125 projects out of 2,732 CDM projects worldwide.

The UK is currently participating in 100 of the 125 CDM projects in Mexico, the majority of these projects with British participation relate to GHG mitigation and Methane recovery.

Chapter 9: Public Private Partnerships Opportunities

There are two main areas of opportunity for British companies within the financial services sector: Public Private Partnerships (PPPs) and listing on the exchanges.

With the help of UK advisers, the Mexican Government introduced a PPP programme based on the UK model. A total of nine Federal PPP projects have been implemented including three hospitals, one university and five road projects. There are ten more Federal PPP projects in the pipeline including six hospitals and four more road projects. At a state level four PPP projects have been implemented, all in the State of Mexico including a cultural centre, a hospital, a road project and a bridge. Mexican companies are keen to form associations with British firms with proven PPP experience in order to participate in these projects.

Plans to extend PPPs further has been reflected in President Calderon's National Infrastructure Plan with projects including prisons, police stations, hospitals, roads and public transport projects.

Listing on the exchanges

Many of the major family-owned conglomerates are reaching the point where they need capital to grow and realise their expansion plans, particularly into the USA market. As they introduce professional management, they are now starting to meet international requirements for accountability and transparency and have begun to list in New York. London offers an attractive alternative.

The Stock Exchange, Alternative Investment Market (AIM) and Plus Markets translate into very appealing solutions for these companies.

Business Opportunities
- PPP's consultants/operators.
- Consortium managers.
- Contract management specialists.
- London Stock Exchange, Alternative
- Arbitration.
- Financial Services

Currently, there are 19 Mexican PPP projects including those already operating, those under construction and some pending for bids.

Chapter 10: Food and Drink Opportunities

Changes to eating habits in a country with a population of over 112 million, rising living standards and the spread of large USA style supermarkets have led to an increase in the importation of foreign foods. The USA, France, Spain and Germany are doing well in this sector as are some British companies.

Beer consumption in Mexico per capita in 2011 was approximately 48.2 litres. There are aprox 65 million potential beer consumers and every year this number increases by about one million (from consumers that reach drinking age). Grupo Modelo and Femsa Cerveza have about 97 per cent of the beer market in Mexico. This has limited the inclusion of foreign brands to between 2 per cent and 3 per cent of the Mexican market.

Unilever, Cadbury Adams and Diageo are clear examples of how UK companies are operating and doing business successfully in Mexico.

Given the size of the market and changes to eating habits, opportunities exist for British companies. There is a continuing increase in imports of foreign food and drinks. As the Mexico is price and quality driven, opportunities exist for both investing in the retail sector and for selling to the market.

Business Opportunities for niche products such as

- Delicatessen.
- Gourmet, and organic foods. Including natural and dietary products.
- Food and drink products reflecting health concerns, weight loss and a healthy way of living.
- Food and drink products that addressing the needs of an ageing population including calcium rich and energy specific products.
- Ready to drink beverages and beer.
- Specialised food and packaging machinery given the need for many companies to renovate existing machinery to satisfy health and safety standards.
- Dairy products and services including refrigeration, packaging and advertising.

With a young population (the average age in Mexico is 26) and a spread of convenience stores around the country are the two main driving forces creating the growth in the confectionery Mexican market. 32 per cent of Mexican confectionery consumption is imported.

300m soft drinks consumed per day!

Mexico is the world's second biggest consumer of soft drinks. It is estimated that the average daily consumption per person is three soft drinks or 300 million soft drinks per day!

Until 2008, Mexico was one of the tougher markets for foreign beers.

There was no presence of UK beers in the market until 2008 when Cervecería Minerva started the distribution of Fullers. Other UK brands now available in Mexico are Charles Wells, Youngs, St Petersand Hobgoblin.

Chapter 11: Healthcare Opportunities

Healthcare provision is a high priority for the current administration (2006-2012). The current President's National Healthcare Programme concentrates on six main pillars: universal healthcare coverage; high care; reinforcement of infrastructure; prevention and promotion of health; a fair and adequate drug policy and an effective and dynamic health regulation.

Budget-wise, the healthcare sector is one of the sectors that has grown the most over the past years, representing 7 per cent of the GDP. In 2011, this sector was allocated the biggest budget in the history of Mexico.

In 2011, the federal budget authorised for the sector was US$11,506 million, with an annual growth rate of 15 per cent between 2006 and 2011.

In addition, the medical device sector in Mexico reached a US$3.58 billion value in 2010 and it is expected to reach a US$6.87 value by 2015.

Within the six pillars, The current President's priority is to achieve universal health coverage, by focusing on the following four areas:
- In 2007 alone, over US$3.39 million was invested in expansion and modernisation.
- A national promotion and prevention strategy.
- Health Caravans, a plan that will provide medical services for the country's most

isolated communities that lack sufficient medical infrastructure, mainly indigenous villages and communities.

- Strategy for supplying medication at health institutions; US$324 million is now available to boost supplies at hospitals and units in the health sector.

UK/Mexico relations in the Healthcare sector are good and Mexico wishes to adopt the NHS model, focusing on the fundamental concepts of free at the point of delivery and universal coverage. Within the Healthcare sector the pharmaceutical and MedTech market have been the most dynamic, offering the most opportunities. This market accounts for approximately 1.21 per cent of the national GDP, generating US$11,376 million; a figure which is constantly increasing.

The medical device sector in Mexico reached a US$3.58 billion value in 2010 and it is expected to reach a US$6.87 billion value by 2015.

In October 18th, 2011, President Calderon announced the new Health Input Regulation Reform representing a significant opportunity for the pharmaceutical industry to develop new medicines and increase their market under the regulation of Federal Commission for Protection from Health Risks (COFEPRIS).

Business Opportunities

- PPPs (Private and Public Partnerships).

- Biomedical products.
- Investment and supply of pharmaceuticals.
- Medical equipment.
- Healthcare promotion.
- Training in PPP hospital management.
- Training in geriatrics.
- Consultancy and training for nurses.
- Consultancy in institutional reform.
- Quality assessment and management.
- Accountability.
- Telemedicine.
- Medical informatics.
- GP training in prescribing team building, management.
- Primary healthcare and paramedics.
- Patient safety.

Chapter 12: National Infrastructure Plan

President Calderón's first objective when his administration started was to make Mexico one of the 30 most competitive economies by 2012. Today, Mexico is the 11th largest economy according to the World Bank's (GDP) ranking, purchasing power parity (PPP).

This achievement can be seen as a result of the National Infrastructure Plan developed in 2007, in which they are planning to invest US$226 billion on infrastructure and an additional US$200-250 billion were allocated to be spent on housing. A significant number of projects have already been undertaken but there are still opportunities for British companies to get involved.

The plan aims to finance transport infrastructure projects; developing roads, railways, airports and ports as well as telecommunications, water supply and sanitation, irrigation and flood control infrastructure, electricity, oil and gas production and refinery, gas and petrochemicals.

In response to the economic slowdown, President Calderón announced emergency spending proposals, which actually include stepping up public spending, especially on infrastructure, including roads, ports, airports, railroads, wind power, hydroelectric plants, water treatment plants, dams, aqueducts, schools, houses and a new oil refinery. The expenditure on these works is for construction, maintenance, modernisation and expansion.

President Calderón's National Infrastructure Plan allocates 5 per cent of Mexico's GDP making it the highest infrastructure investment in history.

In addition to the National Infrastructure Plan, urban development is seen as a priority sector for the Government. Currently there are plans for the development of approximately 20 new satellite cities that include the appropriate social infrastructure to create successful sustainable communities, with adequate infrastructure links to the main cities.

Business Opportunities
- Consulting engineers.
- Facilities managers (roads, ports, airports and railways).
- PPP specialists.
- Equipment and machinery suppliers.
- Roads, ports, airports and railways.
- Security consultants.
- Sustainable technologies.

Mexico currently has 74 airports (11 international and 63 national). 116 ports (116 and 67 coastal high). Approximately 27,000 km of railways. 138 thousand kilometres of paved roads (126 thousand kilometres of two-lane roads and 13,000 km four-lane highways or more).

Roads:

An estimated US$26 billion is expected to be allocated towards building or improving roughly 18,000 kilometers of highways and rural roads. Furthermore the Treasury Ministry announced recent plans to renew four border crossing points in the state of Baja California including an extra 4,000 Km connecting roads to the crossing points.

Ports:

The National Infrastructure Plan aims to modernise Mexico's main ports and create 4 new ports with an estimated US$6 billion investment. Some projects have been completed already like the expansion of the port or Veracruz and the construction of the Specialised Container Terminal in Lazaro Cardenas. The upcoming projects that are yet to be tendered are the multipurpose terminal in Mazatlan and another Specialised Container Terminal in Lazaro Cardenas.

Airports:

Mexico hosts the largest jet fleet in Latin America. Tenders to start new airports are yet to be launched. Nevertheless US$5 billion investments are planned to be allocated to upgrade and expand supplementary airports like Cuernavaca, Toluca, San Jose del Cabo, Merida and San Luis Potosi.

Railways:

Mexico has the third highest volume of freight transport by railways amongst OECD countries. Mexico's railway systems ought to be modernised and there are projects to improve network connectivity; railroad bypasses, bridges and other complementary works. Tenders on the construction of the suburban railway line 3 will be launched soon.

Public spending has increased on infrastructure, including roads, schools, houses, prisons and a new oil refinery.

Chapter 13: Mining and Steel Opportunities

Mexico is a major supplier of metals including silver, ranked first in the world, lead (fifth), zinc (eighth), copper (thirteenth) and gold (fifteenth). Today 279 foreign enterprises are contributing to the investment and exploration of Mexico's mining sector.

Many new investments are beginning to come to fruition. In Mexico the mining extraction sector is second in terms of investment and it sees stable yearly growth.

Steel

Mexico is the thirteenth largest producer of crude steel in the world and the second largest in Latin America with a production of 18.1 million tonnes in 2010 and an installed capacity of 22.2 million tonnes. Mexico has considerable appeal as a steel producer, and factors like receptivity to foreign investment are encouraging major players in steel end-use sectors such as automotive and electrical equipment to establish extensive and sophisticated manufacturing facilities in Mexico. The industry's input cost advantage, which includes labour, electricity and gas, enables it to profitably and competitively export steel products.

According to the 2011 edition of "Ranking of Countries for Mining Investment" by BEHRE

DOLBEAR, Mexico occupies fifth place worldwide in the lowest risks for mining investment table, after Canada, Australia, Chile and the USA.

Since the opening of their Mexico office, steel company Vesuvius has raised its profile and expanded its business in the country. The company, which provides steel makers, foundries and even oil refineries with materials, services and technologies that are used in high-temperature industrial processes, is now working hard to improve its productivity and expand its business in Mexico as more private steel companies move into the area.

Business Opportunities

- Mexico has major opportunities in mineral exploration.
- Mexico has eleven giant deposits of silver, three of copper, two of molybdenum, five of zinc, one of lead, one of manganese and one of fluorite. These deposits represent opportunities for exploration, machinery, tools, consultancy and new technology.
- Companies with expertise in feasibility studies have also big opportunities in the mining sector in Mexico.
- The iron and steel industry in Mexico is experiencing intellectual challenges. Companies are open to R&D that can provide the know-how and knowledge in different fields such as new technologies, composites material, new applications, demand and price forecasting, among others.

- In the next five years, the ironworks sector in Mexico will invest about US$10,000 million to grow and diversify their products, replacing imports.
- Home supplies such as stoves and refrigerators continue to grow in demand; therefore materials such as steel and copper are being required much more.

Chapter 14: Oil and Gas Opportunities

In 2011, Mexico was the seventh largest oil producer in the world and currently ranks among the top 20 in terms of gas production. Petróleos Mexicanos (PEMEX), the State National Oil Company is one of the largest oil companies in the world and the sole producer of crude oil, natural gas and refined products in Mexico, being the most important source of government income.

PEMEX requires resources of around US$20 billion per year in capital expenditure in order to maintain production in declining fields, develop a more efficient exploitation of proven reserves, a move towards deep-water reserves and to increase security and minimise environmental impact.

PEMEX has oil reserves of 45 billion barrels and proven reserves equivalent to 9.2 years of production (13.8 billion barrels) Deep water accounts for more than half of PEMEX's prospective hydrocarbons reserves.

In October 2008, an energy reform was passed by the Mexican Government which means that PEMEX has been granted greater autonomy for decision making. This alleviates some of the previous restrictions and therefore makes the state company more open to do business with foreign companies.

Mexico is the world's seventh largest oil producing country with an approximate production of 2.75 million barrels per day and the world's fifteenth largest oil proven reserves. The country's shale gas potential resources are considered to be among the highest in the world and their development will need the technology and expertise of world class energy companies.

In 2011, British company Petrofac won two of the first three contracts offered by PEMEX to the private sector for performance improvement of the Magallanes and Santuario mature onshore fields located in the state of Tabasco.

Petrofac will invest £303 million for a 90 per cent interest return, it will also receive a reimbursement of 75 per cent of its development costs and extra bonuses for incremental production.

While the great majority of the oil and gas industry is in the hands of PEMEX, there are opportunities for UK companies, particularly with the new contract schemes and also for equipment and service suppliers in specific projects. British firms already participate in Mexico's oil and gas industry, both in the new contracts schemes and as service suppliers.

There is more potential to participate in making Mexico's future deepwater production a safe, clean and efficient one. The UK can share its expertise and experience from the North Sea in areas, such as: project management, major contracting, design and manufacturing of advanced equipment.

In 2010, PEMEX announced and tendered its first incentive based contract model for exploration and production. In 2011, PEMEX tendered the first three incentive exploration and production contracts, won by Petrofac. The first licensing round included the mature onshore fields of Carrizo, Magallanes and Santuario; the second round of mature field contracts is expected to be announced in early 2012 and will include 6 blocks (4 onshore and 2 in shallow waters). The contract model for the second round of tenders is expected to be very similar to the one designed for the first round.

Major UK companies can bid for PEMEX contracts or might explore the possibility of establishing partnerships with current PEMEX contractors where efficient and affordable technology will be the key.

Most opportunities will appeal to innovative and experienced companies in areas such as: productivity, redesign and maintenance of wells, seismic surveys, environmental restoration studies and infrastructure works. UK companies can sell services to the winning contractors or negotiate a consortium.

Business Opportunities
- Onshore and offshore.
- Platform design and construction.
- Decommissioning of production.
- Facilities.
- Design, construction, installation and commissioning of pipelines.
- Receiving terminals and production facilities.

- Exploration and appraisal drilling.
- Production operations.
- Environmental control.
- Regional geological studies (including 3D and 2D seismic).
- Reservoir appraisal and exploration techniques.
- Training and education.
- Deep water technologies.
- Develop heavy and extra heavy oil recovery technology.

Chapter 15: Power and Renewable Energy Opportunities

Mexico's power plays a key role both in the domestic and foreign markets.

By 2014, the country's power generation will account for 21 per cent of Latin America's, with a developing power surplus available for export to the United States.

Also, an annual 4.9 per cent growth is expected in power consumption in Mexico for the period 2006-2016.

The Mexican electricity market grew by 25 per cent in 2008 to reach a value of US$43.5 billion. By 2013, it is forecasted to have a volume of 881.7TWh, which represents an increase of 135.6 per cent since 2008. The annual growth rate in terms of volume, between 2008 and 2013 is predicted to be 18.7 per cent.

There are more than 30 million users, reaching 97 per cent of the population. Mexico had a total power generation of 230,640 GWh during 2009. By 2012, the Mexican electricity market is forecast to have a value of US$80.5 billion representing an increase of 117 per cent since 2007.

Additionally, according to the National Infrastructure Programme, the Mexican Government is planning to increase power generation capacity through renewable resources from 14 per cent to 26 per cent, including hydro power plants, by 2012. A substantial number of projects need to be developed in order to achieve this goal. The current generation of renewable energies amount to 15 TWh, this is expected to go up to 21 TWh by 2014.

Total installed capacity in Mexico is now 51,035MW, including the following sources:

- Independent Power Producers: (11,457MW)
- Hydropower plants: (11,333MW)
- Thermal Power Plants (consuming hydrocarbons): (23,235MW)
- Coal fired plants: (2,600.0 MW)
- Geothermal power plants: (960 MW)
- Nuclear power plants: (1,365 MW)
- Wind-driven power plants: (85 MW)

In 2010, Aggreko, world leader in the supply of temporary power and temperature control solutions, was chosen to provide power for the lights, large-screen plasmas, broadcasting centres, audio equipment, security equipment, and pyrotechnic works for the Bicentennial Celebration of Mexico's Independence.

In 2011, Aggreko supplied a turn-key rental power package to the Pan American Games and the Parapan American Games in Guadalajara. In addition, Aggreko supplied back-up power to the International Broadcast Centre (IBC) in the Guadalajara Expo Centre. Aggreko has also been very successful in selling its temporary power solutions to contractors of the local oil and gas sector. Aggreko currently has offices and depots in Mexico City, Monterrey, Villahermosa, Guadalajara and Poza Rica.

Considering Mexico's privileged geographic location and a stronger legal framework to support private investment in cogeneration, independent power production including renewable energies, small production and self supply, and exporting and importing schemes, the power sector presents unprecedented opportunities for British investors.

Business Opportunities
- Combined cycle plants maintenance and reconfiguration.
- Plants modernisation and maintenance.
- Hydroplants reconfiguration.
- Metering.
- Interconnection projects.
- Transmission and distribution.
- infrastructure.
- Cogeneration projects.
- Renewable energies (small and large hydro, solar, wind, geothermal, biofuels, wave and tidal).
- Financing and carbon markets.

Chapter 16: Mexican Security and Defence Opportunities

The Security sector in Mexico embraces a wide range of activities relating to the Local, State and Federal Government's delivery of crime prevention and investigation, protection of people, property and assets; and law enforcement in general.

Since taking office in December 2006, President Calderón has made security one of his top priorities. A new law on Public Security, aimed at boosting co-ordination between federal, state and public security institutions to reduce corruption and impunity has been ratified. The law also seeks to allow police greater freedom to investigate crime and professionalise the work of the security forces translating in to the creation of the Ministerial Police.

New Federal Security Programmes have been developed that concentrate on civilian security, law enforcement, and serious and organised crime. These programmes include significant budget increases to departments in charge of public security at the state and municipal level; approval of the creation of a National Policing Evaluation Centre and a National Council for Public Security; a new federal law to confiscate goods and properties of organised crime; the creation of a national criminal database register.

G4S, the UK's largest security solutions group, has been in Mexico for more than 30 years, and now have presence and services all over the Country.

Since 2009, they have had an accelerated growth in providing integrated security services to automotive companies, including three of the most important car assemblers worldwide.

Mexico is creating a new Federal Police force with more investigative powers leading to a demand for security products and services. The Federal administration along with a number of State and Municipal Governments are continually assessing assets and where identified, restructuring and replacing current systems by renovating specialised teams and equipment. Innovative technologies will replace outdated systems in a number of areas.

Business Opportunities
- IT infrastructure.
- Automatic license plate recognition systems.
- Voice detection systems.
- Explosive detection equipment.
- Sophisticated CCTV cameras.
- X-ray systems.
- Data management software.
- Mobile phone jammers.
- Sophisticated biometrics.
- Sophisticated anti-riot equipment.
- Security infrastructure developers.
- Training.

Chapter 17: Telecommunications and Video Games Opportunities

Mexican telecommunications is an ever changing and increasingly profitable market. The recent proliferation of wireless communications in Mexico has been so extraordinary that the country is now considered one of the region's most promising markets for wireless equipment and services.

The telecommunications market in Mexico grew 11.1 per cent in 2010. Since 2003 the industry has had an average annual growth of 20.94 per cent according to the Mexican Federal Commission of Telecommunications.

There is a high demand for mobile data, and the 3G uptake will continue to grow in the coming years. In 2010 Mobile phone traffic grew 15.1 per cent, while mobile phone lines grew 9.4 per cent reaching a total of 91.3 millions. On average there are 1.9 mobile phones per household and 80 per cent of households have at least 1 mobile phone. In the case of the internet, Mexico is the second country in Latin America in terms of internet users with 35 million in 2010.

Business Opportunities
- IT equipment for SMEs.
- Integration on wireless connectivity solutions for mobility, VoIP and servers.

- Electronic consumption products such as MP3 players, mobile phones, PDAs.
- Wholesalers are promoting the migration to a specialised model of distribution focused on solutions like consultancy, outsourcing, technical support that can contribute to higher profits.
- There is an expected growth of file, storage equipment, for example USBs and removable hard drives.
- Specific equipment for areas of high growth including multifunction equipment, digital cameras, handhelds, and telecom equipment (voice and data).
- Training in English for the electronics industry.
- Recycling of electronic components.

The Mexican video games market is worth US$400 million per year, and it is the fourth largest market in the world.

Chapter 18: Leisure and Tourism

Mexico holds an important place in the International tourist market which in turn is also very important for Mexico's economy. According to the World Tourism Organisation (UNWTO), Mexico had 22.3 million tourists in 2010 which equated to US$11.8 billion in tourism revenue.

The substantial level of investment (both foreign and domestic) and influx of travellers have shaped the strategy of the tourism industry. New world class developments and competitive prices means there is a shift to target a more upscale market, especially in the Northwest (Sinaloa, Sonora, Baja California Sur and Baja California) where the newest tourism destinations are being developed. Ecotourism, golf and sailing are some of the areas these new developments are focusing on.

In Mexico there are around 220 golf courses and each year more are constructed. According to the Association of Golf Courses for the Mexican Caribbean, by this year they expect to build at least 16 golf courses.

Mexico has a solid marine infrastructure. It ranks among the top ten countries worldwide in terms of ports. Its 5,797 miles of coastline offers diverse opportunities both in the commercial and leisure industry. At present, Mexico relies on 16 main ports, some used exclusively for commercial purposes, yet all of these are part of a broad initiative. Between

2010-2012, the Government plans to invest more than US$700 million in infrastructure and technology to fully exploit the connection between Mexico and the sea.

The betting industry in Mexico has continued its growth, and has become the second largest market in Latin America, recording a total sales revenue of US$639 million in 2010.

The Mexican Government has established a shipbuilding program of coast and ocean patrols with a total budget of US$426 million. The construction program represents 27 per cent of the total budget of the Agency. The Substitution of Naval Units program has a US$152 million budget.

There are many synergies between the Mexican and British sports market and companies can find a large growing market in which to sell their products. The most popular sports in Mexico are: football, baseball, basketball, golf, motor sports, boxing and sailing. Future sporting events being planned and bids will also signal opportunities for British companies looking to supply the local market. In 2011 Guadalajara hosted the Panamerican Games.

Business Opportunities
- Golf course designers, developers, advice on maintenance and construction and training.
- Hotel and resort investors.
- Hospitality technology.
- Sports infrastructure.
- Sports and recreational products.

- Sports apparel.
- Development of marinas.
- Crew training and licensing.
- Navigation and waterway management.
- Safety, rescue systems and insurance.
- Parts, supplies, materials and services related to maintenance and repair of pleasure boats and yachts.
- The betting industry in Mexico has continued its growth, and has become the second largest market in Latin America, recording total sales revenue of US$639 million in 2010.
- Distribution of class II and III slot machines.
- Online and mobile betting platforms (although they have still not been approved).
- Gaming technology and casino related services like consultancy, security.

Chapter 19: European Union Free Trade Agreement

The EU-Mexico Free Trade Agreement allows British companies to export to Mexico without tariff barriers. It aims to allow EU and Mexican goods and services effective access to each other's markets.

In signing the agreement in 2000, Mexico and the EU agreed to progressively liberalise their markets further over the next 10 years. Both the EU and Mexico also committed not to put in place any additional protectionist measures that might affect exports from the EU to Mexico and vice versa.

What does the EU-Mexico FTA mean for you?

As a British exporter, the EU-Mexico Free Trade Agreement provides equal access to the Mexican market that USA and Canadian exporters enjoy under NAFTA. This means British industrial goods and other qualifying exports enter Mexico tariff free. The FTA also guarantees access to public tender offers in Mexico for European companies, provided that the value exceeds certain established thresholds.

For example, a significant proportion of EU cars entering Mexico previously had tariffs imposed of 20 per cent. These tariffs have now been entirely eliminated, making EU cars more competitive on the Mexican market.

The EU-Mexico FTA provides for:

- The progressive and reciprocal liberalisation of trade in goods and services.
- The gradual liberalisation of trade in agricultural products.
- The liberalisation of investment and related payments.
- The opening of markets to public contracting.
- The protection of intellectual property rights

Practicalities British exporters are required to prove that their goods are of EU origin in order to qualify for the benefits of the EU-Mexico FTA. In practical terms this means completing an EUR-1 form and also declaring the origin of the goods on the export invoice.

Chapter 20: Why is Nafta Relevant?

Since the advent of the EU-Mexico free trade agreement, British companies have been able to export to Mexico on equal terms to those enjoyed by USA and Canadian exporters under NAFTA.

But NAFTA may also present advantages for British companies, particularly in the absence of a free trade agreement between the EU and the United States.

By processing or producing goods or parts in one NAFTA country, British exporters may be able to supply all three markets at reduced tariffs or even tariff free.

For example, it might be possible to manufacture part of a product in the UK, export it to Mexico under the EU-Mexico Free Trade Agreement tariff free and then, add parts in Mexico and export the end product to the USA and Canada tariff free under NAFTA.

Non-North American parts should constitute no more than 7 per cent of the total cost of the product. However processing in North America may also change a product's tariff classification and potentially allow it to be imported to NAFTA tariff free.

The treaty allows companies registered in Canada, Mexico or the USA to bid for government contracts in any of the other two countries.

NAFTA also facilitates immigration between the three countries making it easier to transfer workers that are nationals of a NAFTA country to other NAFTA countries.

If transport costs from Europe are high, for example for heavy goods, a British company might consider licensing its technology or establishing an operation in one NAFTA country from which it could export, tariff free, to the other NAFTA markets.

NAFTA has led to the creation of numerous manufacturing operations based in Mexico supplying the USA and Canadian markets, particularly in the automotive, aerospace, food and drink, medical, security and consumer goods industries.

Excellent export opportunities exist for British tier 2 and tier 3 manufacturers who already supply similar operations in Europe to supply these operations in Mexico.

Often these manufacturing operations are set up as maquiladoras. Under this system, goods can be temporarily imported tariff, tax and duty free for use in the production of goods destined for export. So, for example, car parts might be imported tax free to Mexico from the EU, assembled and then exported to the USA with the tariffs only being assessed on what is imported to the USA and no tariffs being paid in Mexico.

In fact, Mexican legislation allows a wide range of goods to be imported tariff free under the maquiladora system including raw materials, parts, packaging, fuels, freight containers, tools, security equipment, machinery, laboratory and investigation equipment.

Service maquiladoras also exist, allowing for packaging or design and engineering to be performed in Mexico for re-export.

The three NAFTA countries form the largest market in the world. In 2007, the GDP of the NAFTA area was around US$16,200 billion.

The population of the NAFTA area is around 440 million. Since NAFTA was signed, there has been a tripling of trade between the three countries. In 2007, there was US$894 billion of trade between the NAFTA countries.

Mexico also has free trade agreements with; Japan, Uruguay, Iceland, Lichtenstein, Norway, Switzerland, El Salvador, Guatemala, Honduras, Israel, Chile, Nicaragua, Bolivia, Costa Rica and Colombia. Similar principles apply in these agreements as apply to NAFTA and the EU FTA.

Mexico also has partial agreements with Brazil, Uruguay, Argentina, Peru, Ecuador, Paraguay and Panama.

Chapter 21: Finding the Right Agent or Distributor

Once you have decided that entering the Mexican market is right for your company, you will need to identify which part of Mexico you will start in unless, of course, you are doing business in Mexico as a result of an initial enquiry from a Mexican company.

To export successfully to Mexico, you will probably need to employ an agent or a distributor. An agent is a company's direct representative in a market and is paid commission. A distributor sells products on to customers after buying them from the manufacturer; their income comes from the margin they can make on resale.

Your agent should be a legally established company, and preferably not an individual (because termination of the agency agreement with an individual can be expensive due to labour laws on severance pay). References should be sought before appointing an agent. They should be obtained from customers of the potential agent and from the companies they represent. In Mexico the business grapevine works extremely well, and the British Chambers of Commerce has a Board of Directors covering a wide variety of fields; who may be able to provide advice as to who is reputable and who is not.

We suggest that, before you grant exclusive rights to a distributor, you seek legal advice.

Once you have chosen an agent or distributor, you will want to ensure that your products receive a fair share (or more than a fair share) of the agent's attention. This can be achieved by:

- Visiting senior management as often as is feasible; this shows interest in, and commitment to, the agent and the market. It helps to develop the all-important personal relationship. It will also provide you with an opportunity to learn about conditions in the market and see how your products are faring.
- Working closely with the agent to show them how they can profit from your products.
- Offering support at regional trade fairs, which can be an excellent way of building distributor loyalty.
- Helping to prepare marketing and sales plans for the agent.
- Providing regular training for the sales staff and after-sales training for the technical staff in the UK.
- Linking performance to incentives and agreeing milestone targets.

Local representation is strongly advisable. In some cases where health certification is required (for example edible products, beverages, toiletries, meat, and medicines and related products), a local agent is a legal requirement.

There are no fixed rules or standard procedures to be followed when finding an agent or distributor in Mexico. Probably the simplest way is to call potential customers who can tell you who is already selling goods to them.

Attendance at exhibitions, both in Mexico and the southern USA, might also help in identifying potential agents. Take your time to find the right agent.

It is important that the agent you appoint is already in contact with the kind of clients you want access to, that they specialise in the products you wish to sell, and that they have experience in the market. It is not easy for one agent to represent successfully a large variety of products or to cover the whole of Mexico. It is important to establish how much of their effort would be devoted to your products. In order to ensure successful national distribution, your agent will probably appoint sub-agents or distributors in the provinces.

Your agent should also be bilingual.

If the market for your products is with public sector agencies, your agent will need to know how to obtain information about government tenders. For your part, you should supply your agent with relevant up-to-date literature in English and Mexican Spanish and provide samples whenever possible. In order to avoid unnecessary difficulty or expense in customs duty and brokerage, you should ask the agent how this material should be sent, and instructions should be strictly followed.

UK companies whose main market is North America and those that are manufacturing or have an input into the manufacture of large or heavy products should investigate whether a Mexican base would improve their competitiveness.

Other companies for whom a permanent presence might be suitable include those that already have manufacturing bases in the USA that wish to reduce costs, as well as UK-approved suppliers to manufacturing companies in the UK or USA, where these companies have a maquiladora or manufacturing presence in Mexico (for example the OEMs such as Sony, Ford, Volkswagen and Nissan).

Mexico is an attractive proposition for UK companies wishing to set up in the market due to its well-established and integrated supply chains, an increasingly skilled workforce, and free trade agreements with 44 countries. These benefits, together with the competitive labour costs and future growth potential, still mean that Mexico is an option that should be seriously considered, not just for the straightforward assembly carried out by the maquiladoras, but also as a base for a more sophisticated manufacturing operation.

The checklist below details things you should bear in mind when looking for a suitable agent or distributor.

Background
- Size of agency
- History of agency
- Number of salespeople, their length of service and qualifications
- Other companies they act for

- Banking and trade references
- What is the core business of the agent or distributor?
- Does the agent or distributor carry products which will compete with yours?
- Does the agent or distributor have qualified staff who can offer the necessary technical support, without which clients will not buy the products?

Distribution

- Geographical coverage
- Types of outlets covered
- Transportation
- Warehousing

Are they right for your product?

- Knowledge of local market conditions
- Marketing competence
- Degree of English language skills throughout the organisation
- Agent's interest in and enthusiasm for new products – and yours in particular
- After-sales service levels
- Required skills of salespeople
- Personal relationship – this is very important in Mexico

Chapter 22: Representative Offices

There are no hard and fast rules about representative offices. The investor climate is friendly and there are few restrictions on the form of business entities a foreign investor can establish. Investment can range from a branch office to a fully owned subsidiary, but most investors set up a corporation or sociedad anónima (SA). This requires a minimum share capital of at least two shareholders and registration in the public register. A sociedad anónima is similar to a limited company in the UK.

All foreign investments must receive prior authorisation from the Ministry of Foreign Affairs. It is essential that you get legal advice from a Mexican lawyer before investing.

A maquiladora (or maquila) is a factory or assembly plant operated in Mexico under preferential tariff programmes. These have been established by the Mexican Government in order to encourage the development of industry in Mexico. This allows materials to be used in maquiladoras to enter duty-free, provided the finished product is then immediately exported out of Mexico. Maquiladoras are also allowed to sell to the domestic market as long as customs duties are paid on the temporarily imported raw materials included within the finished goods sold in Mexico.

The success of the industry lies in the favourable labour market in Mexico, with its relatively low wage rates compared with those in industrialised nations, coupled with Mexico's proximity to the USA. This combination of cheap labour, low transport costs and a favourable tax regime has helped US companies to remain competitive with those from Asia.

Since 1994, this industry has developed significantly and has evolved from a straightforward assembly operation to a more complex manufacturing structure.

Technological institutes have been established, creating a more highly trained workforce, and changes in regulations mean that maquiladoras can now be established anywhere in the country. Supply chain operations – maquiladoras

Chapter 23: Shelter Operations, Joint Ventures and Subcontracted Manufacturing

Another form of maquiladora is the shelter operation. This is often the way foreign companies begin working in Mexico. A shelter operation allows foreign companies to conduct labour-intensive production in Mexico on an outsourcing basis. The shelter operators have the legal exposure to employment law rather than the foreign investor.

This can therefore be a particularly attractive option for small to medium sized companies for which the risks involved in foreign investments are particularly important.

Joint Ventures

A joint venture is as the name suggests; an organisation jointly owned by a Mexican and a foreign partner, and was for a long time the only option available for foreign investment. Joint venture contracts are easily set up in Mexico. Such a contract does not create a business entity and operations are carried out by the active party. However, income and losses are divided between the two partners according to the contract.

Other forms of business identity are normally used when a legal entity is required, for example SA; SA de CV (capital variable), similar to a public limited company; and S de RL (responsabilidad limitada) which is similar to a limited liability company where the partners' liability is limited to the amount of their contribution. Legal advice should be sought to ensure that you choose the right entity for your circumstances.

Federal and state governments offer a number of incentives for companies looking to invest in Mexico, including preferential property positions, tax exemptions and training.

State governments offer these and other incentives on a case-by-case basis and offers are kept private between the investor and the state. Private negotiations may lead to other incentives dependent upon the amount of the investment, the amount of employment created by the new investment; and the economic growth of the region given such investment.

Subcontracted Manufacturing

Mexico provides a good opportunity for UK companies to subcontract the production of manufactured goods, given the lower costs and the availability of skilled labour.

A number of large OEMs have set up in Mexico, due to its proximity to the USA and the existence of NAFTA. This provides UK companies with opportunities to become part of the supply chain for these OEMs, particularly where they form part of the supply chain for these manufacturers in the UK and other markets.

The UK and Mexico have signed and ratified an Investment Protection and Promotion Agreement. This ensures that UK investors in Mexico and Mexican investors in the UK receive "fair and equitable treatment and full protection and security". Among other things, this increases the bilateral protection available to UK and Mexican companies operating in each other's countries, ensures that they will be accorded the same rights as domestic investors, and prevents nationalisation or expropriation of assets without market value compensation.

If you would like an electronic copy of the agreement, please email: mexicocommercial.mexico@fco.gov.uk.

Chapter 24: Due Diligence

Companies employing Mexican nationals should be aware that the law protects employees in a number of ways. In particular, foreign investors should consider payroll taxes borne by the employer, Christmas bonuses and profit distribution.

Due diligence is a security measure that companies often choose to undertake in order to check the viability of potential new business before contracts are signed.

Due diligence is strongly advisable, particularly in connection with the acquisition of a shareholding interest either in a limited liability company or a corporation, and in the acquisition of all quotas of a limited liability company or shares of a corporation.

For practical purposes, it is recommended that due diligence covers all accounting, tax and legal issues concerning a particular business enterprise.

Special attention should be given to ongoing, or threatened, commercial and tax claims at administrative and judicial level.

Due diligence Marketing

You may need to adapt your product to meet Mexican preferences or requirements in order to be able to sell it. Ignoring local regulations, tastes and cultural preferences is a recipe for failure; it's hard to sell a left-hand drive car in a right-hand drive country!

Trade shows, exhibitions and advertising are good ways to attract potential customers. You will need to ensure that your sales literature is effective in both English and Mexican Spanish and consider whether advertising is appropriate.

The language spoken in Mexico is Mexican Spanish. The differences between Mexican and European Spanish are slight and are similar to those between British and American English (ie differing accents and some different words). A basic knowledge of Spanish will always make a good first impression. Correspondence and trade literature should be in Mexican Spanish wherever possible. Although English is widely spoken, there are still many who do not speak it or understand technical terminology. In some cases, it is a legal requirement to label products in Spanish.

It is advisable to engage the services of a local interpreter to accompany you to your first meeting with a potential partner, until it is established whether your partner is confident in doing business in English. The Export Communications Review provides companies with impartial and objective advice on language and cultural issues, in order to help them to develop an effective communications strategy, thus improving their competitiveness in existing and future export markets. Subsidies are available for eligible companies.

If you are thinking about doing business in Mexico, you will need to establish how you can protect your intellectual property rights, how much it will cost and what other steps you could take. An independent intellectual property rights lawyer is invaluable in helping you to establish the best strategy for your company.

Mexico's intellectual property law regulates the use of patents, trademarks, industrial and model designs, trade names, advertisements and business names in Mexico. Under Mexican federal law an administrative body, the Mexican Intellectual Property Institute www.impi.gob.mx, is granted search, seizure and closure powers.

Chapter 25: Banking and Finance

Since 1997, most national banks have been sold off to foreign institutions. The main institutional investors are Citicorp, Scotiabank, Santander, BBVA and HSBC. These banks hold over 80 per cent of total deposits of Mexican savers and over 65 per cent of total financial assets in the system.

Given the stabilisation of inflation rates, the remarkable decrease of Mexico's risk profile, the strict control of monetary aggregates and the firmness of the Mexican peso, financial institutions are competing fiercely to increase their market share in mortgage, retail (credit cards, car leasing or purchase etc) and micro-credit. As a consequence, interest rates are close to their lowest level since 1970.

UK banks are able to offer companies a number of short-term finance options, such as documentary credit, factoring, forfaiting and credit insurance facilities. Details of the available credit options should be obtainable from the international department of your bank.

Tax is a complicated subject and only generalisations can be made. Any income generated in Mexico by non-resident individuals will be taxed by Mexican authorities. The rate varies (between 3 per cent and 33 per cent) according to the level of income. Advice should be sought from a lawyer specialising in these matters.

Chapter 26: Mexican Documentation Requirements.

Tariff Harmonised System code

The Harmonised System (HS) code is an international method of classifying products for export purposes. This classification is used by customs officials around the world to determine the duties, taxes and regulations that apply to the product. For more information on how to obtain your HS code, you should visit: www.businesslink.gov.uk.

Although it is advisable to insert the details of the HS code of the product to be exported to Mexico on the declaration of origin where required, only the first four digits of the HS code should be inserted, as these are common for every country in the world under the HS rule.

Duties and Taxes

EU and Mexico signed a free trade agreement in July 2000. Under this agreement, tariffs were reduced over a seven-year time frame, with all remaining tariffs on EU–produced industrial goods exported to Mexico being eliminated on 1 January 2007. The free trade agreement contains strict rules of origin designed to ensure that only goods of EU origin gain from preferential access to Mexico. VAT, known by its Spanish initials as "IVA", is levied on a variety of goods at 16 per cent.

Commercial invoices

Commercial invoices are required for all shipments to Mexico and must be issued in Spanish or English. By law, all invoices must contain at least the following information:

- Full name, address and tax ID number of supplier
- Full name and address of importer (buyer)
- Complete description of goods (abbreviations are not accepted)
- Quantity of goods being sold clearly shown (if you are sending sets, then you need to include the number of pieces in each one)
- Price of the goods (per unit and total) – in US dollars or Mexican pesos
- Total amount of the invoice
- Declaration of the origin of the goods (EUR1)

All invoices must have the following declaration: "The prices, quantities, descriptions and origin of the goods included in this invoice are sworn to be true and correct".

Approved exporter status

If you are a regular exporter, you may qualify to become an "approved exporter". This means that, subject to HM Revenue & Customs authorisation, you will be able to issue a "no value limit" invoice declaration. This does not need to be presented to Customs, a Chamber of Commerce or Institute of

Chartered Shipbrokers Office for authentication prior to export.

Certificate of origin

A certificate of origin is a document identifying where the product, or parts of it, originates from. The certificate also confirms that the products fulfil the standards established in Mexico and grants a tax preference. There are different types of certificate of origin depending on the goods and services being exported.

The following certificates may require validation from the Mexican Ministry of Economy:
- Sistema Generalizado de Preferencias (SGP)
- EUR1 (Unión Europea y Asociación Europea de Libre Comercio)
- Artículos Mexicanos

EUR1

The EUR1 is a movement certificate and is used to claim zero duty in Mexico. The goods must fully meet the rules of origin and be accompanied by a correctly completed and endorsed EUR1 form.

The EUR1 form should be completed by the exporter. UK chambers of commerce are able to endorse it. The goods must be described in sufficient detail to enable them to be identified and it is recommended that, wherever possible, the descriptions on the certificate and invoice match.

Packaging list

A packaging list is necessary when more than one package is shipped. This document should be sent together with the commercial invoice, and should include: number of packages; a detailed list of the merchandise contained in each package; net, gross and legal weight in metric equivalents; and volume or measurements, in the metric system, of each package. It should also include the total weight of the shipment.

Bill of lading

A bill of lading forms the basic document used in the shipping of goods by sea. It is issued by the ship operator to the shipper (or customer). Three originals and a number of copies are produced, with the copies being kept for reference by those through whose hands the originals pass. One is retained by the master or broker, and the other two dispatched by the shipper to the buyer of the goods, or to the consignee for those goods, if not the buyer. One original will be presented to the master by the customer as evidence of his title to receive the goods. The information on the bills of lading should correspond with that shown on the invoice and the packaging list.

Export licences

Export controls apply to goods upon which the UK Government has placed export licensing requirements. Typically, export controls relate to military items, dual-use goods (civilian goods with a potential military use), radioactive sources, goods of national heritage (such as works of art), and certain chemicals used in the production of controlled drugs.

The Export Control Organisation (ECO) is part of the Department for Business, Innovation and Skills (BIS) under its International Trade Investment and Development Directorate (ITID). ECO issues licences for the export of strategic goods. ECO also issues trade control licences for the trafficking and brokering of arms and dual-use goods. A licence is required if the intended export is listed on either the UK Strategic Export Control Lists or because of end-use controls (which make exports licensable even if not on a control list).

Whether a licence is required depends on various factors, including the type of items exported and any sanctions in force on the export destination.

To determine if your goods need an export licence, you may call BIS ECO's helpline on: +44 (0)20 7215 4594/+44 (0)20 7215 8070.

If you think that your goods may be of importance to national heritage, you are advised to contact the Department for Culture, Media and Sport on: +44 (0)20 7211 6000.

For chemicals that are used in the production of drugs, contact the Home Office at: www.homeoffice.gov.uk.

If the above departments consider your products to be sensitive, you will need to apply for an export licence before you can take them out of the UK.

Dangerous goods

If you consign goods that are classified as potentially dangerous when transported, you must arrange their packing and transportation by air, sea, road, rail or inland waterway, according to international regulations.

The UN Model Regulations harmonise the rules on the various methods of transportation into a classification system in which each dangerous substance or article is assigned to a class defining the type of danger which that substance presents. The packing group (PG) then further classifies the level of danger according to PG I, PG II or PG III.

Together, class and PG dictate how you must package, label and carry dangerous goods, including inner and outer packaging, the suitability of packaging materials, and the marks and label they must bear.

Other regulations define the training and qualifications that dangerous goods drivers and safety advisers must hold, and when you must use one.

More detailed information on documentation requirements and import procedures can also be found at the Market Access Database, (http://madb.europa.eu/), HM Revenue & Customs (www.hmrc.gov.uk) or Business Link: (www.businesslink.gov.uk).

The Market Access Database is a free tool designed to assist exporters:

- It provides information on trade barriers which may affect you in overseas markets.
- The Applied Tariff Database section allows users to enter an HS code or product description to obtain a tariff rate and details of taxes applicable, enabling you to calculate a landed cost.
- The Exporter's Guide to Import Formalities database (searchable by HS code or by product), gives an overview of import procedures and documents, as well as any general and specific requirements for a product.
- The Sanitary and Phytosanitary Export Database facilitates the identification of sanitary and phytosanitary export problems with any non-EU country.

The Market Access Database can only be accessed through an internet service provider based in the EU.

Chapter 27: Certification and Standards

Different regulations apply to different sectors, so it is difficult to be specific without going into enormous detail. The best source of information for UK exporters is the EU's website at: http://madb.europa.eu. From here you can select Mexico as a country and see what restrictions have been placed on the products in your sector. As general advice, ask your importer what documents and licences or certification your product needs; they will have detailed and up-to-date knowledge.

Certificates of Free Sale

A Certificate of Free Sale is required for certain products to show that goods are available for retail sale. The documents are guarantees to the importing country that the UK product is no risk to consumer health. For more details, please telephone:

- BIS +44 (0)20 7215 5000 – cosmetics, chemicals, detergents and cleaners, disinfectants.
- Defra +44 (0)8459 335577 – food, drinks, additives, disinfectants, pesticides, animal medicines, milk and dairy products, pet food and animal feed, fertilisers, sugar and sugar products, protein crops, tea, coffee, cocoa, herbs, spices, tobacco flavouring and wines.
- Department of Health +44 (0)20 7210 4850 medical, dental and surgical equipment and prostheses.

- Medicines and Healthcare products Regulatory Agency (MHRA) +44 (0)20 3080 6000 – medicinal products.
- Health and Safety Executive (www.hse.gov.uk) – pesticides, fertilisers and hazardous or toxic substances used in the manufacture of these products.
- Forestry Commission +44 (0)117 906 6000 – phytosanitary certificates for products or packaging material made out of or containing wood.

Details in Spanish of products requiring Certificates of Free Sale are available at: www.cofepris.gob.mx.

Health certificates

All suppliers into the healthcare sector must have local representation. Products for the healthcare market require a "Sanitary Registration" issued by COFEPRIS (Comisión Federal Protección para la contra Riesgos Sanitarios), a devolved agency of the Ministry of Health.

USA or European standards and registrations, although helpful, are not sufficient. All products that require a Sanitary Registration must have a Mexican company or individual responsible for them. A Sanitary Registration is issued in the name of the distributor. The main documents required for product registration are:

- A Certificate of Free Sale issued by the NHS.
- A Certificate of Quality

- A Letter of Appointment of Distributor. These three documents must be in Spanish and translated by a legal translator. Technical information may be in English with a summary in Spanish.

The whole process takes about six to eight months. The COFEPRIS website (www.cofepris.gob.mx) gives full details in Spanish. There are also specialist consultants who are experienced in advising on registration matters.

Further details on the process of obtaining a Mexican health certificate can be obtained from the UK Trade & Investment team in Mexico.

Labelling requirements

Mexico's labelling requirements are often different from the EU's. In most cases, exporters have to attach special labels to products they are sending to Mexico even if the products are already labelled in Spanish.

NOM-50

NOM-50 is an official Mexican standard which refers to the commercial information of the product that the foreign company has to provide. The label must include a description of the goods, together with:
- The name of the importer.
- The name of the exporter.

- A declaration in Spanish that the goods have been made in the UK: Hecho en Reino Unido.
- The quantity of pieces that each packet contains.
- A Mexican Registro Federal de Contribuyentes form from the importer.
- Tax ID from the exporter.
- Reference to the need to use a manual if use or conservation requires.
- Expiration date, when necessary.

This procedure is sometimes costly to fulfil in the country of origin but importers (or manufacturers) can pay for the services of a verification unit. Verification units are third-party individuals or private companies accredited and approved to conduct compliance assessments and ensure the conformity of labels with the relevant official norms.

Importers may submit each shipment to a private verification unit. The use of verification units is voluntary but this procedure does simplify fulfilment of Mexican requirements. Verification at the border ensures that the product fulfils the specific technical requirements when it is sold in Mexico.

The verification units charge

US$200–250 per "dictamen" (control of a label). Each dictamen covers one product or a family of products and thus the verification price of a shipment containing many different items or models is very high. More information on Mexican labelling standards is available from the British Standards Institute. Contact details are provided in the section on technical help for exporters opposite.

Technical standards

Certain products, goods, processes and services must comply with the technical standards issued by the Mexican Ministry of Trade. NOMs (Normas Oficiales Mexicanas) are Mexican standards that some imported goods need to meet before they can go on sale in Mexico. There are three main types of NOMs: security, labelling and emergency.

All relevant standards and technical regulations can be found at the official website at: www.economia-noms.gob.mx/noms/inicio.do.

Technical help for exporters

This service is provided by the British Standards Institution (BSI) to give information and advice on compliance with overseas statutory and other technical requirements. BSI produces a wide range of publications and provides a special updating service of information in some product fields. BSI can: supply detailed information on foreign regulations; identify, supply and assist in the interpretation of foreign standards and approval procedures; research and give consultation on technical requirements for a specific product; and provide translations of foreign standards, items of legislation and codes of practice. Fees vary according to the amount of work involved.

For specific enquiries, contact BSI on:
Tel: +44 (0)20 8996 9001
Fax: +44 (0)20 8996 7001
Email: cservices@bsigroup.com

Chapter 28: Mexican Customs Regulations

Mexican customs law regulates the flow and transport of goods to and from Mexico. Goods may only pass to and from Mexico at authorised locations. Customs authorities monitor the entry, exit, transport and control of goods. Merchandise must be presented to the customs authorities together with the required documentation.

There is a 0.8 per cent customs processing fee charged by Mexican customs, based on the cost, insurance and freight (cif) value of the goods.

Mexico requires the intervention of a customs broker to clear merchandise through customs when the total value of the shipment is more than US$1,000. Details of customs brokers are available from the UK Trade & Investment team in Mexico.

Commercial samples and temporary imports

Samples of no commercial value and those rendered valueless may be imported free of customs duty. Samples which are of value are subject to the appropriate duties or may be imported under a bond that guarantees their re-export within one year. An extension to this can be applied for from the Director-General of Customs in Mexico City.

Professional tools and equipment can be imported temporarily by those with business visas, provided they do not exceed the value of that which a Mexican could own in similar circumstances. However, customs officials have the discretion to decide whether or not such a temporary import is bona fide. If, for any reason, they suspect that it is not, they may either confiscate the article or place it in bond.

It is always advisable to use the services of an authorised customs broker at the port of entry and also at the port of exit. Their services can be obtained through international forwarding agents.

Chapter 29: Pricing, Insurance and Getting Paid

Pricing should be competitive and price lists should be in US dollars or Mexican pesos. Mexican Spanish should be used, if possible, and all costs should be included.

Insurance

The private sector provides credit insurance for exports of consumer goods, raw materials and other similar goods. Speak to your banker or insurance broker for more information, or contact the British Insurance Brokers' Association for impartial advice. It can be contacted at:
British Insurance Brokers' Association 8th Floor
John Stow House
18 Bevis Marks
London EC3A 7JB
Email: enquiries@biba.org.uk
Website: www.biba.org.uk

Private sector insurance has some limitations, particularly for sales of capital goods, major services or construction projects that require longer credit packages or that are in riskier markets.

Commercial risk insurance for capital goods and major projects

UK Export Finance is the UK's official export credit agency. Its aim is to help UK exporters of goods or services to win business and complete contracts with confidence. UK Export Finance can support contracts valued as low as £20,000, and potentially up to hundreds of millions of pounds. The responsibility for providing insurance cover for consumer goods that are sold on credit of less than two years rests with private sector insurers.

UK Export Finance provides services such as:
- Insuring UK exporters against non-payment by their overseas buyers;
- Helping overseas buyers to purchase goods and/or services from UK exporters by guaranteeing bank loans to finance those purchases.
- Sharing credit risks with banks in order to assist exporters in the raising of tender and contract bonds, in accessing pre- and post-shipment working capital finance and in securing confirmations of letters of credit.
- Insuring UK investors in overseas markets against political risks.

UK Export Finance works closely with exporters, sponsors, banks and buyers to put together the right package for each contract. The full range of UK Export Finance facilities are available to support exports to, and investments in, Mexico.

To help those customers relatively new to exporting, UK Export Finance has a customer service team dedicated to helping new customers through the process of credit insurance and export finance. For more detailed enquiries, please contact UK Export Finance's customer service team on: +44 (0)20 7512 7887 or Customerservice@ecgd.gsi.gov.uk.

Getting paid

When exporting to Mexico, normal commercial rules should be followed. Companies should discuss arrangements on the security of payment with the international department of their UK bank or the UK branch of a bank operating in Mexico.

If you are a first-time exporter to Mexico, the standard method of receiving payment for your goods is by a Letter of Credit or by payment in advance.

A Letter of Credit is a form of contract between two banks. A bank will make payment provided that the documents submitted to it are in strict compliance with the conditions of the Letter of Credit regardless of the purchase contract. To prevent the possibility of a payment being made if the terms of the purchase contract are not met, the seller should check the Letter of Credit against the terms of the purchase contract and request amendments from the buyer if necessary.

The opening of the Letter of Credit is based on the contract signed between the buyer and the seller. There are no problems regarding Letters of Credit opened by Mexican banks being accepted by foreign banks. The Mexican bank will make payment provided that the requirements of the Letter of Credit are met.

Due to the cost and delays associated with Letters of Credit, many Mexican businesses will wish to move to open account terms once a trustworthy relationship has been developed between the two parties.

Major exports and those requiring long-term finance will require specialist payment and financing.

Before conducting business in Mexico, UK business people should be aware of the local customs that need to be taken into account.

Chapter 30: Status and Greeting Etiquette

Mexican companies and government departments are hierarchical and status conscious. Most decisions are made at the top and representatives will be received by somebody fitting their status. If you send junior sales representatives, they will not meet the main decision-makers.

Greeting etiquette

Mexicans attach great importance to titles. Professional titles such as "Licenciado" (meaning "graduate") or "Ingeniero" (engineer) should be used as this recognises their status. Those without titles should be addressed with Mr (Señor), Mrs (Señora) or Miss (Señorita) followed by their surname.

When doing business in Mexico, you will find that first names are not always used initially as they are reserved for family and close friends. Wait for someone to address you by your first name before doing so yourself.

Men and women will shake hands when they meet for the first time in business and social situations. If they already know somebody from a previous meeting, men tend to greet men with a hug/shoulder slap and both men and women greet women with a kiss on the right cheek.

On departure, you should repeat all the handshaking and kissing, and it can take 10 minutes to get out of a room!

Time for this should be included in your programme; don't assume that you will be able to make a quick exit.

Meeting etiquette

- In Mexico, business attire is more formal than that in the USA or Europe. It is therefore important to be well dressed for business meetings. This means dark suits, long-sleeved shirts and usually cufflinks for men and lightweight dresses for women.
- Business is personal in Mexico. Before doing business, try to ensure that you have contacts who can introduce you or vouch for you. Once an initial contact has been made, it is easier to move on and arrange future business meetings.
- Make business appointments in advance and confirm them with a brief phone call a few days before. Once you arrive in Mexico, call again or send an email or fax to ensure it is known that you will definitely be arriving.
- Timekeeping is relaxed in Mexico. However, due to the Mexicans' long-established business links with Europe, they are used to European business people being on time, so will also try to do the same. When having an appointment in Mexico City, always consider the traffic as it may affect your schedule.

- Business cards are usually exchanged at the beginning of the meeting. It is useful to have business cards printed in English on one side and in Mexican Spanish on the other. Consider having this done before arriving in Mexico.
- Mexicans don't like to cause offence and this can extend to not wanting to say "no". Not saying "no" doesn't necessarily mean "yes".
- Substantive business will only be done in person. The telephone is limited to making arrangements.

Meetings and greetings

There are two forms of interpreting. Consecutive interpreting means that you speak and then your interpreter interprets. This is the usual form for meetings, discussions and negotiations. Simultaneous interpreting is when you speak while the interpreter interprets simultaneously; but special equipment is required which is expensive to hire. Simultaneous interpreting is generally used only for large seminars and conferences, and there are always at least two interpreters who will interpret in 20-minute sessions.

Interpreting is a skill requiring professional training. Just because someone is fluent in English and Spanish, it does not mean that they will make a good interpreter.

If you are giving a speech or presentation, remember that the need to interpret everything will cut your speaking time approximately in half (unless using simultaneous interpreting). It is essential to make sure that the interpreter can cope with any technical or specialist terms in the presentation. It is better to be slightly restricted and speak close to a script than to fail to be understood because your interpreter cannot follow you. If you are giving a speech, give the interpreter the text well in advance and forewarn them of any changes.

Below are a number of recommendations for getting the best out of your interpreter:

- Though expensive, a well-briefed professional interpreter is best.
- Try to involve your interpreter at every stage of your pre-meeting arrangements. The quality of interpretation will improve greatly if you provide adequate briefing on the subject matter. Ensure that your interpreter understands what you are aiming to achieve.
- Speak clearly and evenly, without rambling on for several paragraphs without pause. Your interpreter will find it hard to remember everything you have said, let alone interpret all your points.
- Conversely, don't speak in short phrases and unfinished sentences. Your interpreter may find it impossible to translate the meaning if you have left a sentence hanging.
- Avoid jargon, unless you know your interpreter is familiar with the terminology.
- Take into account that some interpreters may be more familiar with American English and

have a little difficulty at first with British accents.

- The UK Trade & Investment team in Mexico can provide a list of specialist translators.
- Avoid making or telling jokes. These almost invariably fall flat in translation and will confuse or embarrass your audience. Compliments or observations could be a more effective icebreaker.

Interpreters

Sophisticated PowerPoint presentations with multiple illustrations are the norm for many forward-looking Mexican companies, and it is advisable to take the same approach to create a good impression. Handouts and brochures in Mexican Spanish are recommended.

Never start a presentation apologetically. During presentations avoid slang and jokes specific to British culture and geography. Your Mexican audience may not understand. There is no need to be extremely formal. Do not speak too quickly, loudly, or in a monotonous tone.

At the beginning of the presentation, make it clear to the audience whether you prefer to take questions during or after the talk. Often, audiences are happier writing down their questions rather than asking them in front of others.

If there is not enough time to take all written questions, tell the audience that you will reply to them by email and do so.

Mexicans prefer doing business with people who they know and trust. Your success in Mexico is therefore dependent upon your ability to establish, build and maintain good relationships. Interpersonal skills are needed to fit in, cultivate relationships and win the favour of others. These can actually be more important than professional experience and know-how.

Learning Spanish is obviously of benefit. If you don't have time to become conversant, making the effort to learn basic pleasantries can go down well. The differences between Mexican and European Spanish are similar to those between British and American English (i.e. with differing accents and some different words) so if you speak European Spanish you should be understood. Joining the British Chamber in Mexico will give you access to a network of other businesses.

Chapter 31: Business Entities

Mexico is composed of 31 states and a Federal District. The states are free and sovereign, divided both administratively and territorially into local governments having their power.

There are different structures that investor's may use, as desired, for investment vehicles in Mexico. They range form setting up a commercial corporation or a branch to forming a joint venture or a trust.

Companies

The General Corporation Law recognizes the existence of six types of commercial organizations or structures. However, in daily corporate practice in Mexico, the types of companies most utilized are:
(a) limited liability stock corporation or "sociedad anónima" and
(b) the limited liability company or "sociedad de responsabilidad limitada".

Any of these types of companies may be organized with variable capital which allows the business to alter its capital (the variable portion) with a minimum of formalities.

(a) The Limited Liability Stock Corporation or "Sociedad Anónima"

The "sociedad anónima" is the most used and accepted business structure in Mexico. It operates under a company name and ownership is in the form of shares in the capital of the company.

Shareholders' liability is limited to making capital contributions to the company for the purchase of shares.

The creation of a sociedad anónima requires a minimum of two stockholders and a minimum share capital of not less than Pesos $50,000. The authorized capital must be fully subscribed within one year of the establishment of the company. The management of the corporation is entrusted to a sole administrator or a board of directors.

(b) Limited Liability Company or "Sociedad de Responsabilidad Limitada"

The limited liability company is one formed by members whose obligations are limited to the payment of their contributions to the capital of the company, but in which ownership interests cannot be represented by negotiable certificates, either in "registered" or "bearer" form. Such contributions are transferable only in the specific cases provided by the General Corporation Law.

After the limited liability stock corporation, the "sociedad de responsabilidad limitada" is the most commonly used business structure in Mexico, and may be considered for United States tax purposes as a partnership.

A limited liability company may not have more than 50 members. The capital of the company may never be less than Pesos $3,000 which must be divided into "parts" or "interests" which may be unequal in value and rights but must always represent one peso or a multiple of such amount.

To incorporate any of the types of business organizations, the charter and articles of incorporation require formalization by a notary public and thereafter, registration with the Public Commercial Registry, thereby constituting notice to the world of the incorporation.

The Branch of a Foreign Corporation

The General Corporation Law provides that a foreign company has legal existence and is entitled to set up branches in Mexico when it is recorded in the Public Commercial Registry in the location where it intends to set up the branch. It must obtain the prior authorization of the Mexican Departments of Foreign Affairs and of the Economy. In order to obtain such authorizations, among other requirements, the foreign company must prove that it has been incorporated in accordance with the laws of its country and that its charter and by-laws contain no provisions that are contrary to Mexican law.

In order to obtain authorization from the Department of Foreign Affairs to open a branch office, it is necessary to file a notice in which the company waives its right to invoke the protection of its government in matters related to the acquisition of ownership of property within Mexico.

Trust or "Fideicomiso"

In accordance with Mexican law, a trust is a contract whereby a person, known as the settler, makes use of certain property for a specific lawful purpose, entrusting the achievement of the purpose to a trustee. The person benefiting from the trust is the beneficiary. Business may be carried out through a trust.

In Mexico, only banks and certain other financial institutions may act as trustees. Individuals or legal entities other than such banks or the specified financial institutions are prohibited by law from acting as trustees with the exception of stockbrokers in connection with the investment of trust funds in securities.

Chapter 32: Foreign Investment Regime

Pursuant to the Foreign Investment Law, any Mexican corporation or partnership with foreign shareholders or partners may engage in any business or participate in new fields of economic activity or manufacture new product lines, open and operate establishments and enlarge or relocate already existing establishments, provided the corporation or partnership does not engage in economic activities reserved for the state or Mexicans, whether individuals or corporations, or is subject to other specific restrictions. The only requirement is that otherwise applicable laws and regulations be observed.

Mergers, Acquisitions, and Business Combinations Mergers

There are two different kinds of mergers provided for in the General Corporation Law:

- A merger in which simultaneously a new company is created and one or more merging companies lose their separate legal existence, and
- A merger in which one or more companies are absorbed into the surviving company.

Any merger of Mexican companies must be approved by the shareholders in an extraordinary shareholders meeting of each of the companies involved which must then be notarized and recorded with the Public Registry of Commerce in order to have legal effect.

Acquisitions

Under Mexican law, it is possible to acquire a business by:

- The purchase of or subscription for shares of stock in a company or
- The purchase of the assets of the business.

Business Combinations

The current regulatory framework relating to business combinations in Mexico consists of the following laws:

- The Federal Antitrust Law.
- The Foreign Investment Law.
- The General Corporation Law.
- NAFTA and other treaties to which Mexico is a party.

Prior notice to the Federal Antitrust Commission of combinations, joint ventures, mergers and acquisitions may be required, depending upon the amount involved, in order to comply with the Federal Antitrust Law.

Antitrust / Anti-Competition Law in Mexico

The Federal Antitrust Law is intended to promote free competition and regulates concentrations, as well as absolute and relative monopolistic practices, in a similar way to antitrust law in the United States upon which Mexico's antitrust law is based.

The Commission may penalize concentrations and monopolistic practices as follows:

- Order the suspension, alteration or ending of a concentration or monopolistic practice.
- Order the reverse, partially or totally, of a concentration.
- Levy fines on those engaging in prohibited activities.

Chapter 33: Real Estate

The Mexican Federal Civil Code provides that any sale of real property exceeding the equivalent of approximately, Pesos $21,900.00. Will have to be formalized in writing before a public notary therefore, any sale of real property requires compliance with that formality.

Furthermore, the notarial deed transferring title to real property requires registration with the Public Registry of Property of the place where the real property is located or the sale will not be effective with respect to third parties. It is important to point out that federal law also provides that the offices of the Public Registry of Property are to be located in the seats of the judicial districts of each Mexican state. There is therefore no single federal Public Registry of Property, but rather numerous offices around the country where real property and related matters are recorded.

In view of the above, before purchasing any real property, a search in the Public Registry of Property should be carried out as part of the due diligence review.

Foreign Investment Considerations

With respect to title to, and use and enjoyment of real estate, the Mexican Foreign Investment Law provides for a special legal frame work to allow foreign investors to acquire and enjoy real estate in the so-called "Restricted Zone" (100 kilometers along land borders and 50 kilometers along the coastline), as follows:

(a) The acquisition of real estate by Mexican business entities with foreign shareholders:
- Outside the Restricted Zone: Real estate may be acquired without any restriction.
- Within the Restricted Zone: For residential purposes: title to and enjoyment of real estate may be acquired only through a trust, where the trustee holds direct title but the foreigner has the right to use and enjoy the property.
- For non-residential purposes: real estate may be directly acquired, provided such acquisition is registered with the Department of Foreign Affairs ("SRE").

(b) Foreign individuals and foreign business entities.
- Outside the Restricted Zone: Real estate may be directly acquired, with the SRE's prior authorization.
- Within the Restricted Zone: For residential purposes and non-residential purposes: real estate may only be acquired and enjoyed through a trust. The duration of a trust for the purpose set out above is 30 years but may be extended to a maximum of 50 years. As can be seen, real estate in the Restricted Zone to be used for industrial and tourist purposes may be held directly by Mexican entities with foreign shareholders without the need for a trust. Existing trusts may be cancelled in order for such entities to own real estate directly.

(c) Deemed approval

Permits are to be approved or disapproved by the SRE within 30 business days following the filing of the application and registrations are to be approved or disapproved within 15 business days following the filing thereof, failing which, the permit or registration will be deemed granted.

Real Estate Transfer Taxes

In many states, the acquisition of real estate is taxed. The scope of this tax usually encompasses all transfers of real estate and rights thereto. Transfer taxes are borne by the entity that becomes the owner of the property, whether by virtue of purchase, donation, inheritance, in-kind capital contribution, merger, spin off, liquidation, etc. The tax rates range between 2% and 4.8% of the apprised value of the property or the transaction price, whichever is higher.

Chapter 34: The Tax Regime

Mexican corporations (according to Mexican tax law, other legal structures such as asociaciones en participación are also considered as corporations for tax purposes) are under an obligation to pay income tax at the rate of 28% (30% from 2010 through 2012; 29% in 2013; and 28% again as of 2014 of net profits. Net profits are obtained by deducting from all taxable income earned in the fiscal year, the deductions authorized by law. The law authorizes, among other things, the deduction of the cost of the sale of goods and expenses as well as "investments."

Should the amount of the authorized deductions exceed the amount of gross income, a tax loss is incurred which may be carried forward up to ten years and set off against profits in those years.

Mexican taxpayers are required to file annual tax returns which must be filed within the three months following the closing date of the fiscal year. In Mexico, the fiscal year runs from January 1 to December 31.

During the fiscal year, corporations must calculate monthly estimated tax returns which are credited against annual income tax. No provisional payments have to be made during the fiscal year of incorporation.

Single Rate Business Tax

As of 2008 a new tax came into effect, named Impuesto Empresarial a Tasa Única ("IETU") (Single Rate Business Tax). This new tax is introduced as a new a minimum tax, supplementary to income Tax.

This tax applies to individual and entities residents in Mexico as well as to foreign residents with a permanent establishment in Mexico in connection with sales of goods, provision of independent services and lease of goods. This tax would apply to tax payer´s net income at the rate of 17% (17.5% as of 2010).

Exemptions would apply to certain transactions, such as sales of shares, as well as to certain entities, such as charities, provided that certain requirements are met.

The base for this tax is determinate by deducting from the gross income certain items related to the activities levied by this tax, such as expenses associated to purchasing goods, rendering independent services and lease of goods, or those in connection with the administration of such activities. Certain items that are deductible for income Tax purposes will not be deductible for IETU purposes, such as salaries, royalties paid to related parties or interest (except in very few cases).

In addition, certain tax credits are available to offset this tax, namely:
- Income Tax effectively paid on the same fiscal year.

134

- Credit Salaries (excluding fringe benefits).
- Credit for a tax losses.
- Monthly IETU payments.

Value Added Tax

In general terms, value added tax is paid at a rate of 15% (16% as of 2010) by those who sell goods, provide services, grant the temporary use of goods, or import goods or services into Mexico. Value added tax must be passed on to the person who in turn acquires the goods or receives the services until it is finally paid by the ultimate consumer. In the zone along Mexico's land borders, value added tax is payable at a 10% rate (11% as of 2010).

Taxation of a Branch or Permanent Establishment

A branch operating in Mexico usually constitutes a permanent establishment in Mexico. In general terms, tax treatment applicable to a permanent establishment is basically the same as for a Mexican corporation and it must comply with various tax requirements arising from its operations in the country, such as filing income tax returns and issuing invoices meeting tax requirements, among others.

Profits obtained by the establishment will be subject to a 28% (30% from 2010 through 2012; 29% in 2013; and 28% again as of 2014). Profit is calculated by deducting from all taxable income earned in the fiscal year attributable to the permanent establishment, the deductions applicable to the operations of the permanent establishment, whether amounts have been paid in Mexico or abroad. Only income earned from business carried out by the permanent establishment is deemed income attributable to the permanent establishment and subject to corporate tax in Mexico.

Foreign tax residents having no permanent establishment in the country are under an obligation to pay taxes in Mexico only on income earned from Mexican sources.

Finally, it is noteworthy to mention that permanent establishments must also pay IETU in connection with income attributable to it.

Taxation of Dividends

If dividends are paid out of profits on which the company has already paid corporate income tax, such dividends are tax-free in Mexico. For this purpose, companies are entitled to create an "after tax profits account" or "Cuenta de Utilidad Fiscal Neta" ("CUFIN"). Once the applicable corporate tax has been paid, any dividend or profit distribution made from this account is not subject to further taxation regardless of the nationality or residence of the recipient. If corporate income tax has been not paid on the profits used for the dividends, then the corporation must pay a dividend tax, on a grossed up basis, and then apply the 28% corporate rate (30% from 2010 through 2012; 29% in 2013; and 28% again as of 2014). No tax withholding is applicable regardless of the tax residence or nationality of the recipient.

Tax Treaties

Mexico has entered double taxation agreements with several countries. Some of these countries are: Germany, Australia, Austria, Argentina, Barbados, Belgium, Brazil, Canada, Korea, Chile, China, Denmark, Ecuador, Spain, United States, Finland, France, Greece, Indonesia, Ireland, Iceland, Israel, Italy, Japan, Luxembourg, Norway, New Zealand, The Netherlands, Poland, Portuguese Republic, United Kingdom, Czech Republic, Russia, Singapore, Sweden, Switzerland, Romania, The Slovak Republic).

The treaties are usually based on the Organization for Economic Cooperation and Development ("OECD") Model Convention and provide tax relief to avoid double international taxation.

Chapter 35: Intellectual Property Regime

Trademarks

Mexican law recognizes the following types of trademarks:
  (i)   Names and figures.
  (ii)   Three dimensional forms; and
  (iii) Trade names

In order to obtain the registration of a trademark, a written application must be filed with the Mexican Industrial Property Institute (the "Institute"). If the application is properly completed, it is examined in depth from both a formal and novelty standpoint to verify whether the trademark is eligible for registration in terms of the Industrial Property Law ("IPL").

The Institute issues a certificate of registration for each accepted application as evidence of having granted a trademark registration. Registration of a trademark is valid for ten years, beginning on the date of filing of the registration.

The owner of a trademark must request a renewal of a trademark registration within the six months prior to its expiration date although without having to demonstrate its continuous and uninterrupted use. However, an affidavit must be filed as well, stating that the use of the name has not been interrupted for a period of more than three years.

Registration will lapse when the trademark is not renewed or when it is not used for a period of more than three consecutive years, unless there are justified reasons for the lapse in use.

Licensing of Industrial Property Rights

The trademark owner or its recorded licensee is entitled to use a trademark. A license agreement must be recorded with the Institute to protect trademarks against improper use by third parties.

Technology Transfer Agreements

Technology transfer under Mexican law seeks to harmonize Mexican policy with international intellectual property practices. Major breakthroughs of the IPL are the introduction of express protection for industrial secrets with heavy penalties for piracy as well as the patentability of pharmaceuticals.

Patents

Among points of particular interest, the IPL introduces the concept of a "modelo de utilidad", translated as an "industrial model" which is defined as "objects, items, apparatuses, or tools which, as a result of a change in formation, configuration, structure or form, have a function or usefulness different from their constituent parts."

Protection of usable models and industrial designs is achieved by registration with the Institute, which grants the right to use a model for ten years and a design for fifteen years from the date of application. Protection will not be extended at the end of such periods.

The IPL defines non-patentable items specifically only with respect to "living materials."

Copyright

The Federal Copyright Law protects the rights of the authors of any intellectual or artistic work. A copyright is effective during the author's life plus 100 years after his death. Works may be registered at the General Copyright Bureau and provides full protection for the author.

Editors of intellectual or artistic works, newspapers and magazines and the producers of movies or similar publications may reserve the right to the exclusive use of the original graphic characteristics of such works, provided they are different from the work or collection itself.

Reservation of Exclusive Use Right

Periodical publications and broadcast, human or fictitious or symbolic characters, persons or groups engaged in artistic activities and advertising promotions may be registered as "reservation of exclusive use rights, to use and exploit, exclusively, titles, names, denominations, distinctive physical and psychological characteristics, or original operation characteristics applied, in accordance with their respective nature.

Computer Software

Computer software may be registered with the General Copyright Bureau and provides full protection for the creator.

Franchising

The IPL establishes that a franchise exists when a trademark license includes know-how and technical assistance to enable the franchisee to deliver goods and services in a manner consistent and uniform and in accordance with the operating, commercial and administrative methods (policies and procedures) established by the trademark owner (franchisor), all for the purpose of maintaining quality, good will and the image of the products/services.

Franchise agreements must be registered with the Institute for purposes of existence to third parties.

Enforcement

The IPL contains broad protection of intellectual property rights and makes enforceability of these rights more efficient and faster. Under the IPL, patents and trademarks are protected for periods of twenty and ten years, respectively. In addition, protection is given to trade secrets, infringement of which is considered a criminal offense which may result in imprisonment of two to six years.

In general terms, the IPL severely penalizes unfair competition and any type of infringement of intellectual property. Seizure of goods is available as a means of immediately stopping an infringement without having to obtain a prior decision from the Institute or an investigation by the public prosecutor. This seizure is carried out by the Institute.

Chapter 36: Employment

Mexican labour law recognizes and protects the basic unalienable rights of employees, regulates employer-employee relations, and establishes the working conditions for employees.

Basis of Employment Relationship

The Federal Labour Law ("FLL") defines an employment relationship as the providing of a subordinated personal service by one person to another, in exchange for the payment of a wage and in accordance with an individual employment agreement.

The principal element of any employment relationship is subordination, which the Fourth Chamber of Mexico´s Federal Supreme Court of justice has defined as the employer´s legal right to control and direct the employee and the employee´s corresponding duty to obey the employer. Once and employment relationship exists, all the rights and obligations under the Federal Labour Law automatically apply, regardless of how the agreement is characterized by the parties.

The employment agreement should set forth the conditions under which it is to be performed. The employment agreement must state:

(1) The employee's and the employer's name, nationality, sex, civil status and address.

(2) Whether the employment agreement is executed for a specific job or term, or for an indefinite term.

(3) A description of the services to be provided.

(4) The place where the work is to be performed.

(5) The length of the work day.

(6) The wage or salary specifying the day and place of payment.

(7) The training program for the employee pursuant to the procedures and programs established by the employer as required by the FLL, and

(8) Other terms and conditions of employment, such as days off and vacations agreed upon by the employee and the employer.

The employer is responsible for the execution of the agreement; nevertheless, not having a signed agreement does not deprive the employee of entitlement to his or her rights under the FLL.

Duration of Employment

Any individual employment relationship is subject to the principle of "job stability", that is, subject to the employee's right to keep his or her job as long as the employment relationship so requires. If the employment relationship is for an indefinite term, the employee cannot be laid off without cause.

If the relationship is for a specific job or term, the employee may keep his or her job until the specific task is completed. The FLL assumes, as a general principle, that employment is for an indefinite period of time, unless the nature or the particular type of service to be provided calls for an employment agreement for a specific job or term. An employment agreement for a specific period of time may be executed only if the work to be performed so requires it or if the worker is hired to temporarily substitute for another employee.

Dismissals

There is no concept of employment-at-will in Mexico and an employer here may dismiss an employee without liability only if there is a cause for the dismissal, as established in the FLL.

An employee may appeal his or her discharge to a conciliation and Arbitration Board, within two months of the dismissal. The employer has the burden of proof the conduct referred to above and described in Article 47 of the Federal Labour Law. If the employer fails, to prove such conduct the employee can request either.
(1) Reinstatement in his or her previous job, or
(2) A constitutional indemnification equivalent to three months full salary, including premiums, bonuses, commissions, etc., and all fringe benefits. The employee also has the right to receive back salaries, which are the salaries not received by the employee from the termination date until the final ruling from the labour board has been complied with.

The employer is not obligated to reinstate an employee if the employee worked for the employer for less than one year, if the employee must work in direct and constant contact with the employer.

If a normal working relationship is impossible, or if the employee provided domestic services or worked on a temporary basis. If the employer does not reinstate the employee, the employer must pay the employee a lump-sum indemnification equal to three months daily aggregate, salary plus twenty days daily aggregate, salary for each year of seniority.

Employees dismissed with or without cause, as well as those who resign with fifteen or more years of seniority, are also entitled to a seniority premium, equivalent to twelve days salary for each year of service provided; the seniority premium, however may not exceed the twice the minimum daily, salary in effect in the economic zone where the employer is located (plus prorated vacation, vacation premium, and year-end bonus as described below).

In Mexico City, the current daily minimum wage is pesos $57.46, which is equivalent to approximately US$4.50 per day.

The Social Security Law and Worker´s Housing Fund Law

In addition to the FLL, there are other general laws that regulate employment relationships in Mexico, such as the Social Security Law and National Worker´s Housing Fund ("INFONAVIT")

Collective Bargaining Agreements

Employees and employers may also enter into collective bargaining agreements. Collective agreements are executed by one or more employee unions with one or more employers or one or more employer associations.

Either party may request an annual review of the wage scale, and every two years, a review of all other provisions of the collective bargaining agreement.

The provisions of the collective bargaining agreement cover all employees regardless of the union membership. Management employees, however, may be expressly excluded. Although management employees are allowed to have their own collective bargaining agreements, as a practical matter, no unions for such employees exist.

Right to Strike

The Federal Constitution guarantees the employee right to strike. The FLL, however, makes strikes relatively undesirable for both management and employees by establishing limitations on the right to strike and by prohibiting employers from hiring permanent replacements, from operating during strikes (except for essential safety services), or from locking out employees. A strike must have one of the following objectives:

(1) To attain a balance between worker and employer rights.
(2) To pressure the employer to execute, revise, or comply with a collective bargaining agreement.

(3) To force compliance with the employer's obligation to pay profit sharing to the employees.
(4) To annually obtain higher wages; or
(5) To support a strike at another business aimed at achieving any of the above-mentioned objectives.

The union is required to file with the Conciliation and Arbitration Board a strike notice prior to the planned strike and which the Board must forward to the employer within twenty-four hours of receipt. The notice should state the union's demands, its intention to strike, and the strike objective.

The strike may not commence until the employer has been given at least six days' notice prior to the date of the planned strike (ten days if public utilities are involved).

The employer must file a written response within forty-eight hours of receipt of the notice. The Conciliation and Arbitration Board then holds a hearing to try to seek a settlement. The parties may agree to postpone the commencement of the strike in an attempt to reach a settlement.

Within 72 hours after the strike begins, the employer may request that the Conciliation and Arbitration Board declare the strike illegal. The Board will do so if the strike has an unlawful objective or lacks majority support. Both parties are given an opportunity to be heard. If the Board determines the strike to be illegal, employees must return to work within twenty-four hours or risk termination.

Profit Sharing

Employees (other than a chief executive officer), whether or not they are Mexicans, are statutorily entitled to a portion of the employer's profits. The rate of profit sharing is determined every ten years by a National Profit Sharing Commission consisting of worker representatives, employers and the government. The rate for profit sharing is currently 10% of the employer's taxable income as defined by the Mexican Income Tax Law. It is important to point out that newly incorporated companies are exempt from the profit sharing payment during the first year of operation.

Chapter 37: Immigration Security Interest Law

Compliance with Mexican immigration requirements is one of the starting points for doing business in Mexico, since such requirements establish that it is not possible for a non-Mexican to do business of any kind in Mexico without having a visa.

Foreign nationals may enter Mexico either temporarily to conduct business or to live and work, provided they are in possession of the appropriate visa authorizing the activities that they will carry out while in Mexico. It is also important to bear in mind the substantial discretion that Mexican immigration authorities have in applying immigration law and regulations and the information provided below should be viewed with this limitation in mind.

Mexican immigration policy classifies foreign nationalities into three groups:
- Unrestricted
- Regulated
- Restricted,

Different rules apply to each of the category. Regardless of the category, the available visas are the tourist (FMT), business (FMN), FM-3 or FM-2 visas.

The "FMN" business visa allows non-Mexican business people to visit Mexico to, among other things, hold business meetings, negotiate, have meetings with officials from Mexican businesses, or provide technical assistance to a specific Mexican company. It does not permit the holder to be paid by a Mexican company for any activity performed in Mexico.

Security Interests under Mexican Law

The types of security interests that may exist in property under Mexican law are:

Pledge

A pledge agreement provides a personal property right to secure
- The payment of an obligation as well as
- The preferential right to such payment.

In case of a breach by the debtor of the obligations secured by the pledge, the creditor may sell, following the proceedings established by law, the pledged assets and apply the proceeds to the payment of the secured obligations.

Mortgage

A mortgage grants in favour of a creditor (mortgagee) a right over property, whose possession remains with the mortgagor, to be paid out of the proceeds of the disposition of the property in the event of a failure to comply with the obligations being secured. A mortgage is generally established over real estate but can also be granted over personal property attached to real property and over businesses or ships.

Surety Bond

A surety bond is an agreement by which a guarantor agrees to pay the obligations of a debtor in the event the debtor does not do so.

Guarantee Trust

This type of trust is a contract whereby a settlor transfers to a trustee the ownership of certain property in order to secure compliance with an obligation owing to the creditor or beneficiary. In Mexico, only banks and certain other financial institutions may act as trustees.

Equipment or Operating Loan

By virtue of this kind of contract, the debtor is obligated to use the exact amount of the loan for the acquisition of raw materials and equipment as well as for the payment of wages, salaries and the direct expenses of operations indispensable for the business.

This type of loan is secured by the raw materials or equipment acquired with the loan proceeds or the products or manufactured goods resulting therefore.

Financing Loan

There are multiple uses for this type of loan:
- To purchase tools, instruments, farming implements, fertilizer, cattle, or breeding stock.

- To develop farms or raise crops, either seasonal or permanent.
- To open land for cultivation.
- To purchase or install machinery and construct or develop working equipment necessary to carry out the debtor's business.

These loans are secured, simultaneously and separately, with the assets and the products and proceeds, whether future, pending or already obtained, of the business for which the loan was obtained.

Creating and Perfecting Security Interests

A security interest is perfected when all of the applicable steps required by law have been taken, generally, when the security agreement is signed. Registration in the appropriate Public Registry of Commerce and/or Property is required in order to ensure and preserve the priority of the interest being granted.

Chapter 38: Environmental Law in Mexico

Mexican regulations applicable to environmental protection represent a complex system that may be difficult to comply with and may give rise to the imposition of penalties on individuals or companies for failure to comply.

The Federal Department of the Environment and Natural Resources ("SEMARNAT") is principally responsible for environmental protection in Mexico and is similar to the United States Environmental Protection Agency ("EPA"). There are two agencies of SEMARNAT having environmental responsibility, the Environmental Regulations and Promotion Office, in broad terms having responsibility for permitting, and the Federal Environmental Enforcement Agency ("PROFEPA," to use its initials in Spanish), as the name implies, having responsibility for enforcement.

SEMARNAT is concerned, among other matters, with issues related to industry, as follows:

- Encouraging the protection, restoration, and conservation of natural ecosystems and resources, to ensure their sustainable development.
- Guiding national policy regarding national resources and the environment, urban

development, environmental regulations, mining and fishery development.

- Establishing, in conjunction with other federal authorities as well as state and municipal authorities, Mexican Official Standards on the preservation and restoration of the environment and natural ecosystems, the appropriate use of natural resources, waste water discharge, and the safe management of hazardous material and hazardous wastes,

- Evaluating and approving environmental impact assessments and environmental risk assessments for development projects proposed by public, social, and private sectors, as well as evaluating and approving environmental accident prevention programs.

- Managing, controlling and governing the use of water considered as federal property such as basins, reservoirs, rivers, and springs and federal zones including beaches and river banks.

- Granting contracts, concessions, licenses, permits, authorizations and assignments in protected areas, waters, and for forests and mining as well as the use of beaches, federal marine and land zones, etc.

The Environmental Regulations and Promotion Office prepares and evaluates all general policies on environmental matters, issues environmental standards and guidelines, grants licenses and permits of a federal nature, and publishes the Ecological Gazette.

There are a number of permits, approvals and reports, federal or state, concerning environmental matters which must be obtained to operate an industrial plant in Mexico and/or filed during the course of such operations, among them are:

- Environmental impact authorization;
- Operating license or one step environmental license ("LAU," to use its initials in Spanish);
- Environmental Annual Report ("COA," to use its initials in Spanish);
- Registration as a generator of hazardous waste followed by subsequent reports concerning production, transport, and disposal of hazardous wastes,
- Water use concession if the company is going to use water from wells or any other source not provided by a municipal or state water board;
- Wastewater discharge applications and registration.

PROFEPA's main activity is to deal with complaints, conduct inspections and, in general, verify compliance with all federal environmental laws and regulations. It also imposes penalties for violations of environmental laws and regulations and monitors compliance with any preventive and mitigating measures issued by it.

PROFEPA also conducts environmental audits. From the effective date of NAFTA, an environmental cooperation commission made up of a Council, a Secretariat and a Joint Public Consulting Committee was been in existence in order to promote cooperation between the three member countries on:

- Making effective environmental laws;
- Compliance with such laws and their regulations; and
- Technical cooperation

In view of the rapidly changing and complex nature of Mexican environmental legislation, any corporation planning to do business in Mexico or engaging in a new field of activity to review compliance with the legal and technical implications of its activities should exercise care. With respect to industrial facilities currently in operation, the conduct of periodic environmental audits, both of a legal and technical nature is highly recommended in order to avoid potential penalties resulting from inspections by PROFEPA and/or state and local environmental authorities.

Chapter 39: Foreign Trade Law

The Foreign Trade Law has as its purpose controlling and promoting foreign trade, increasing competitiveness in the domestic economy, improving the efficient use of the country's productive resources, properly incorporating the Mexican economy into the international marketplace, and contributing to improvement in the welfare of the international community.

The Foreign Trade Law also deals with tariff and non-tariff regulations and restrictions (such as quotas, import permits and Mexican Official Standards or NOM's) as well as rules on unfair foreign trade practices (antidumping proceedings) and the administrative proceedings held in accordance with internationally accepted practices and mechanisms.

These regulations vary depending on the specific imported product and its country of origin, for this reason, it is imperative to review requirements before deciding to initiate the import/export operations of a company in our country.

The North American Free Trade Agreement

The NAFTA became effective in Mexico as of January, 1994. NAFTA contemplates the establishment of a free trade zone that includes Canada, the United States and Mexico. The objectives of NAFTA consist generally of:

- Eliminating tariffs, obstacles to foreign trade and facilitating the circulation of goods and services between the three signatory countries.
- Promoting competitive conditions as well as capital investment in the members; adequately protecting intellectual property rights.
- Creating efficient procedures for the resolution of commercial disputes between the parties, as well as between their nationals.
- Establishing policies for trilateral and multilateral regional cooperation as well as seeking to broaden the benefits and scope of NAFTA.

With respect to tariff elimination, the three countries accepted diverse "speed of tariff phase outs" concerning goods entering their markets and originating in the NAFTA region.

As of today, almost every single product that qualifies as having NAFTA origin is now free from the payment of customs duties.

The provision of rules allowing importers to certify goods originating in the free trade zone is considered another beneficial aspect of NAFTA due to the application of the preferential treatment granted by Mexico as a NAFTA country.

The IMMEX Programs

The IMMEX Program (in-bond or contract manufacturer) is a federal export promotion program, authorized by the Department of the Economy, which allow Mexican companies, including subsidiaries of a foreign company, to temporarily import into Mexico raw materials, machinery and equipment necessary to manufacture products specified by the foreign company that will be totally or partially exported abroad.

The Executive Order for the Advancement of the Manufacturing, Maquila and Export Services Industries (IMMEX) came into effect on November 1, 2006, As a result, Maquiladora and PITEX programs were merged into the IMMEX program. Companies with IMMEX programs are indistinctively referred to as IMMEX companies or maquiladoras.

The IMMEX programs may benefit companies by exempting them from the payment of import duties on imported raw materials having a NAFTA origin as well as the payment of value added tax. Temporary imports of machinery and equipment and non-NAFTA raw materials under the IMMEX program, do not attract payment of value added tax, although in some cases (non-NAFTA products) import duties are payable, unless the company can take the benefit of a Sector Promotion Program [Programas de Promoción Sectorial] ("PROSEC") as explained below.

PROSEC Program

The PROSEC program was created by the Department of the Economy to neutralize the effect on domestic industry of the coming into force of Articles 303 and 304 of the NAFTA. These articles apply to imports of raw materials, machinery and equipment not originating in Canada, United States, or Mexico. Basically a PROSEC allows its holder to import, on a permanent basis, raw material, parts and components, as well as machinery and equipment under preferential tariffs, provided that such items be used for the manufacture or assembly of the products mentioned in the applicable PROSEC, whether or not the final products are intended for export or for sale in the domestic market.

This program is especially useful when importing goods from non-NAFTA countries when such goods are incorporated in products and then exported to a NAFTA member.

The goods that can be imported, as well as the final products to be manufactured, are organized in twenty-four specific industry sectors, which include, among others, the electric al/electronic, furniture, textile and apparel, footwear, toy, metallurgic, chemical, pharmaceutical, agricultural, automotive and transport industries, among others.

Special Importation Requirements

In addition to the foregoing, with respect to some types of goods intended to be imported or exported, the importer must be registered as such with the Treasury Department not only on a general importers registry but also on the register applicable to the particular product being imported. This additional registration is required for products that may affect the Mexican public health or security.

Finally it is important to mention that, depending in the tariff item classification of the imported product, the importer must comply with the specific tariff (duties) and non-tariff regulations (import permits, Mexican Official Standards, etc.) mentioned before.

Chapter 40: Transportation and Aviation Law

Foreign investment in a company engaged in any of the following businesses is permitted up to a maximum of 25% of its total capital:

- Domestic air transportation,
- Air taxi transportation, and
- Specialized air transportation.

The above percentages cannot be exceeded, either directly or indirectly, for example by using a trust.

Foreign investment however it is permitted without restriction in companies engaged in international air transportation as well as private non-commercial air transportation.

Air transportation in Mexico is predominantly regulated by the Civil Aviation Law ("CAL") and the Air Transportation Law Regulations. The purpose of the latter is to clarify certain aspects of the CAL such as the requirements that must be complied with in order to obtain the concessions and permits necessary for operating air transportation services in Mexico.

The legal framework applicable for concessions and permits is, in brief, as follows:

The federal Communications and Transportation Department ("SCT") is responsible for granting concessions and permits to provide air transportation services.

Concessions are granted to provide domestic scheduled public air transportation services and may only be granted to Mexican corporations complying with the foreign investment limitations previously mentioned.

Such concessions may be for a period of up to 30 years, and may be extended several times for the same period, if the concession holder has fully complied with its obligations under the concession during this period.

Foreign corporations are not allowed to provide domestic transportation.

Permits are granted to provide:
- Domestic non-scheduled services (inclusive of charter and taxi flights),
- International scheduled services.
- International non-scheduled services (inclusive of charter and taxi flights).
- Private commercial services (inclusive of specialized air transportation flights).

A permit to provide domestic non-scheduled air transportation services will only be granted to Mexican corporations complying with the foreign investment limitations previously mentioned.

Permits, however, for operating international scheduled air transportation services as well as international non-scheduled air transportation services and private commercial air transportation may be granted to both Mexican and foreign corporations. All of these permits are issued for an indefinite period.

Airports Law

Companies having foreign shareholders may invest in Mexican airports and aerodromes provided that no more than 49% of the total capital stock of the company is in foreign hands. Nevertheless, companies having foreign investment exceeding this amount may so invest if an authorization from the Foreign Investment Commission is first obtained.

The Airports Law and the Airports Law Regulations that deal with the concessions and permits that may be granted by the SCT predominantly regulate airports in Mexico. Concessions may only be granted to Mexican corporations for the administration and operation, and if applicable, for the construction of airports. Such concessions may be in effect for up to 50 years, and may be extended several times for the same period, provided that the concession holder has fully complied with its obligations under the concession during this period.

Permits may be granted to Mexican individuals or corporations for the operation of private aerodromes and only to Mexican corporations for the operation of public aerodromes. In either case, these permits may only be granted for a maximum period of 30 years. This period, however, may be extended.

Ground Transportation

Foreign investment in entities engaged in domestic ground transportation, whether of passengers, tourism or cargo, is prohibited and the business is exclusively reserved for Mexican individuals or corporations. However, this prohibition does not include the provision of courier services.

Foreign investment in corporations engaged in the provision of international ground transportation either of passengers, tourism or freight, has no restriction, in accordance with NAFTA.

The provision of ground transportation services on highways and federal roads in Mexico is predominantly regulated by the Federal Roads, Bridges and Motor Vehicles Transportation Law and the Motor Vehicles Transportation and Auxiliary Services Regulations.

The SCT is responsible for granting permits to provide ground transportation services, as well as for the installation of interior load terminals and verification units, and for the provision of courier transportation services, among others. These permits are issued for an indefinite period of time.

Railways

Foreign investment in companies that provide public railway services is permitted up to a maximum of 49% of total capital stock. This percentage may be relaxed, however, by a favourable resolution from the Foreign Investment Commission.

Railway transportation service in Mexico is predominantly regulated by the Railway Service Regulatory Law and by the Railway Service Regulations.

These laws establish that a concession granted by the SCT is required to provide public railroad transportation, a concession may be in effect for up to 50 years, and may be extended several times for the same period, provided that the concession holder has fully complied with its obligations under the concession during such term.

In addition, the SCT may grant permits for the provision of ancillary services such as:
- Passengers terminals,
- Cargo terminals,
- Transfer of liquids,
- Maintenance workshops,
- Supply centers for the operations of railroad equipment.

Notwithstanding the above, a concession holder may provide the abovementioned services without the need to obtain a further permit.

Maritime Law

Foreign investment in companies engaged in any of the following businesses is permitted up to a maximum of 49% of their capital stock:

- Companies engaged in the provision of pilotage services for internal navigation in Mexico.
- Ship-owners engaged in domestic or internal navigation, with the exception of tourist cruises and machinery, equipment and other items used in naval construction, conservation and seaport operation.

For the following activities, while companies having more than 49% of their capital stock held by foreign shareholders may generally not engage in the provision of such services, it is possible to obtain an authorization from the Foreign Investment Commission to do so:

- Companies engaged in the provision of seaport services to vessels within internal waters of Mexico, such as towage and moorage.
- Ship-owners engaged in international navigation.
- Maritime transportation services in Mexico are predominantly regulated by the Navigation Law and the Navigation Law Regulations.

The legal framework applicable for maritime transportation services is, in brief, as follows:

- Mexican and foreign companies are allowed to provide international sea-going navigation services.
- However internal and domestic navigation can only be carried out by Mexican corporations or individuals with Mexican

ships, although a temporary 90 day permit may be obtained either by a foreign ship owner operating a foreign vessel or a Mexican ship owner operating a foreign vessel, provided that there is no Mexican ship with the characteristics required for the provision of the particular service.

In addition to the above, a permit granted by the SCT is mandatory in order to provide the following services:

- Passenger transportation and tourism cruises.
- Nautical tourism.
- Salvage, security or assistance navigation with special vessels.
- Towage, maneuvers in port, unless an agreement with the seaport administrator has been concluded.

Ports Law

Companies having foreign shareholders holding up to 49% of the capital stock may act as port administrators.

This percentage cannot be exceeded, either directly or indirectly. Ports in Mexico are predominantly regulated by the Ports Law and the Ports Law Regulations.

The legal framework applicable for concessions and permits is, in brief, as follows:

- The SCT is responsible for granting the concessions and permits necessary for operating ports, terminals and marinas.
- Concessions for ports administration can only be granted to Mexican corporations with the foreign investment limitations previously mentioned.
- Concessions for operating a marine terminal located outside a port, and permits to provide ports services may only be granted to Mexican individuals and corporations.
- Concessions may be in effect for up to 50 years, and may be extended once again for the same period, provided that the concession holder has fully complied with its obligations under the concession during this period.

Chapter 41: Telecommunications Law

Telecommunications in Mexico has changed to allow limited private or foreign investment. This increase in private investment has both driven and reflected rapid growth in the sector.

Foreign Investment Law restricts foreign investment in telecommunications to 49% of the capital of Mexican companies operating in the telecommunications sector.

Activities to which this restriction applies are the use of radio / electromagnetic spectrum in Mexico, the installation and operation of public telecommunications networks, the occupation of positions in space by satellites and the emission and reception of signals from foreign satellites. The restriction on foreign investment does not apply to cellular telephone operations.

Foreign investors may invest in the capital of Mexican companies engaged in the restricted businesses referred to above provided they do so as minority shareholders or hold shares with limited voting rights, and in either case, agree to consider themselves as Mexican nationals with respect to their interest in the company and not to invoke the protection of their own government in the event of a dispute, under penalty of forfeiting their interest to the state for violation of the agreement.

The Federal Telecommunications Law is the governing law in Mexico that regulates the use of the radio-electric band, telecommunications networks, and satellite communications. Subject to the restrictions mentioned above, any individual or company may obtain a concession to provide the following services, among others:

- Public local and long distance telephone service.
- Data transmission.
- Restricted television.

Chapter 42: Energy and Natural Resources

Mexico is a country rich in natural resources including petroleum, silver and copper. As of December 2007, proven crude oil reserves stood at more than 14,717 billion barrels and natural gas proven reserves stood at 18,077 billion cubic feet (Hydrocarbons' Reserves as of December 31, 2007, issued by Pemex).

According to the Mexican Constitution, the state has direct ownership of the subsoil with the result that ownership of natural resources belongs to the state and may not be transferred to private individuals or entities.

The state has the exclusive right to exploit and develop petroleum and gas and may not grant oil exploration and exploitation rights to private entities or individuals. In addition, the generation, transmission, distribution and supply of electricity for public consumption are also reserved for the state.

Mining

The mining industry in Mexico is under exclusive federal jurisdiction and while, as mentioned above, the state has direct ownership over mineral resources, Mexican individuals and companies may obtain concessions for their exploration and exploitation, granted by the Department of the Economy.

Electricity

As provided in the Constitution, the federal government exclusively carries out the generation, transmission, distribution and marketing of electricity that is supplied for public consumption. As of December 23, 1992, the following are not considered as "public consumption" and, therefore, are open to the private sector with no foreign investment restrictions (but subject to obtaining a permit):

(i)   Cogeneration.
(ii)   Self-supply.
(iii)   Independent power production.
(iv)   Small power production.
(v)   Power for exportation.
(vi)   Importation of power.

Public, local and municipal institutions are also allowed to generate electricity for use in public lighting, pumping water, and other public services.

The Energy Regulatory Commission ("ERC") is the body responsible for regulating the energy industry in general and specifically for granting permits, as well as supervising compliance with permit terms.

Oil and Gas

As previously mentioned, the state has direct ownership of the subsoil, as well as the exclusive right to exploit and develop petroleum, including natural gas. As a result, the state may not grant oil exploration and exploitation rights to either private entities or individuals. The agency used by the federal government to exercise its rights in this area is the state oil company, Petroleos Mexicanos ("Pemex"). Pemex may carry out those activities within its responsibility directly or by hiring third parties.

With respect to the construction of pipelines for transportation of petroleum and petroleum by-products as well as oil and gas drilling, approval from the Foreign Investment Commission is required in order for a company having foreign investment exceeding 49% of its capital to carry out the same.

The retail sale of gasoline is exclusively reserved for Mexicans and Mexican corporations that exclude foreign shareholders.

Natural Gas

While natural gas production is exclusively reserved for the state, private investment, including foreign, is allowed in the transportation, storage, distribution and marketing of natural gas in Mexico, subject to obtaining a permit from the ERC.

Liquefied Petroleum Gas

Private investment is allowed in the storage, transportation and distribution of liquefied petroleum gas, subject to obtaining a permit. Permits for transportation and distribution by pipeline are granted by the ERC, while permits for transportation and distribution not by pipeline are granted by the Department of Energy. Transportation and distribution of liquefied petroleum gas, however, is exclusively reserved for Mexicans and Mexican corporations that exclude foreign shareholders.

Energy Reforms (2008)

The constant low level of oil extraction and production, as well as decreasing market prices, contributed to motivate Congress to approve a series of legislative proposals in 2008 that will give Pemex the tools to be more efficient, something which will hopefully result in greater scope for better decision-making. Such energy reforms were intended to modernize and improve the gas, oil, and bio-energy industries in Mexico, allowing greater participation by the private sector, and strengthening of the organization and operation of Pemex.

The content of such reforms may be summarized as follows:

(i)   New methods for contracting to allow additional compensation for the contractor when Pemex benefits from early project completion, benefits from new technology provided by the contractor, or because of other circumstances attributable to the contractor.

(ii)   The creation of a National Hydrocarbons Commission with the technical capacity to regulate and supervise the exploration and extraction of hydrocarbons.

(iii) Providing the ERC with greater authority and technical, operational, management, and decision-making independence.

(iv) Allowing the participation of independent directors in Pemex and the hiring of private contractors through a more simple and expedited process, different from that applicable to all other government entities.

(v) Creation of the following committees:

(a) Evaluation of Development.

(b) Investments and Strategy.

(c) Acquisitions, Leases, Works and Services.

Chapter 43: Reorganization and Bankruptcy Proceedings

Reorganization and bankruptcy have become interesting subjects in Mexico as a consequence of the economic and commercial changes that the country has passed through in the last five years.

In order to adapt the reorganization and bankruptcy legal framework to deal with the economic problems faced by businesses, on May 12, 2000, the Commercial Bankruptcy and Insolvency Law ("CBIL") was published on the Federal Official Gazette. The CBIL only applies to businesses.

According to CBIL, there are two successive stages or phases in insolvency proceedings:
- Reorganization or conciliation
- Bankruptcy.

The reorganization stage is aimed at the preservation of the company or of the business (the "Debtor") through the execution of a reorganization agreement between the Debtor and its creditors.

The bankruptcy proceeding is aimed at selling the assets of the Debtor in order to pay its creditors.

Reorganization Phase

A Debtor which is insolvent and does not comply with its payment obligations, may be declared to be insolvent and thus in the reorganization phase of the proceedings, at the request of the Debtor, its creditors, or the public prosecutor. The CBIL considers that general non-compliance with payment obligations occurs when the Debtor:

- Has debts past due for 30 days, representing 35% or more of the total of the Debtor's obligations on the date the petition for the declaration of insolvency is filed.
- The Debtor does not have assets to meet at least 80% of its past due obligations.

The reorganization stage (as well as any subsequent bankruptcy) is dealt with by a District Court judge of the domicile of the Debtor. Once an application for a declaration of insolvency is made, the Federal Institute of Insolvency Experts (the "FIIP") must then appoint an examiner that will determine whether the Debtor is actually insolvent and then submit a report to the Court that will then decide whether to issue a declaration of insolvency. Once such a declaration is issued, the FIIP then appoints a conciliator, whose principal task is to seek an agreement between the Debtor and its creditors.

The reorganization stage is supposed to take no more than 185 calendar days to be concluded, calculated from the date of the last publication in the Federal Official Gazette of the declaration of insolvency.

The reorganization stage may be extended up to two consecutive times, for ninety calendar days each, on the understanding that this stage and its extensions may never exceed one year.

Effects of the Insolvency Declaration

The most important effects of the insolvency declaration are:

- The suspension of creditor debt enforcement proceedings during the reorganization stage.
- The separation of third party property from that of the Debtor.
- The maintenance of the management of the business by the Debtor (however the conciliator may request the removal of the Debtor and appointment of a receiver in order to protect the assets of the Debtor.
- The creation of a special regime for the treatment of the Debtor's obligations.
- The requirement that creditors prove amounts owing to them.
- The dealing with fraud to the detriment of the Debtor's creditors.

Reorganization Agreement

The reorganization agreement must contain a schedule of payments of the amounts owing to proven creditors and must be signed by all proven creditors, except for tax and employment creditors, representing more than 50% of:

- The amount of all general creditors.
- The amount of all secured creditors.

The reorganization proceeding are terminated when the Court approves the reorganization agreement filed by the conciliator.

Bankruptcy

A Debtor is considered bankrupt, when:
- The Debtor so requests it.
- The reorganization period and any extensions have elapsed without the approval of a reorganization agreement by the Court.
- The conciliator requests a bankruptcy declaration and the Court grants it.

Bankruptcy Declaration

The decision containing the bankruptcy declaration, among others:
- Suspends the legal capacity of the bankrupt to exercise its rights over its property.
- Requires the Debtor and those who have in their possession property of the bankrupt, to deliver to the trustee in bankruptcy, such possession and the administration of the estate in bankruptcy.
- Prohibits the Debtor from making payments or delivering its assets to others.
- Orders the FIIP to appoint the conciliator as trustee.

Effects of Bankruptcy Declaration

The main effect of the bankruptcy declaration is to transfer the administration of the property of the Debtor from it to the trustee, the latter having the same powers and obligations as the conciliator had. Once bankruptcy is declared, the trustee sells the property of the Debtor, trying to obtain the best price for it.

Payment to Proven Creditors and Conclusion of the Proceedings

Payment to creditors are to be made in the following priority:

(i)   Creditors holding a special privilege (funeral expenses of a deceased Debtor)

(ii)   Creditors holding a pledge or mortgage.

(iii) Creditors holding a special privilege (as defined in the CBIL).

(iv) General creditors (without security or privilege).

The proceedings conclude when:

- The reorganization agreement made between the Debtor and its creditors is approved by the Court.
- Total payment is made to proven creditors.
- While payment is made to proven creditors, no other assets are left to be transferred and the estate of the bankruptcy is not enough to make a total payment of proven indebtedness.
- If the Debtor and all proven creditors so request.

Chapter 44: Legal Protection for the Foreign Investor

Mexico's Federal Constitution makes no distinction between foreigners and nationals with respect to the protection of individual rights set out in it, any individual or company is entitled to enjoy such guaranties, regardless of nationality or place of incorporation, in the case of a company.

One of the guaranties established in the Constitution is that no one can be deprived of life, freedom, property, possessions or rights without due process of law. Such due process must be carried out before courts of competent jurisdiction and pursuant to applicable law.

The Commercial Code ("CC") is a federal statute that generally regulates commercial transactions and establishes that, provided the subject matter is lawful, the parties to a contract may freely agree upon the terms and conditions of their choice. The CC also provides that the provisions of the Federal Civil Code apply to all commercial transactions when the CC and other commercial laws are silent on a particular issue. The parties to a contract are also free to agree upon the court or courts having jurisdiction in the event of a dispute under their agreement. They may also agree to submit to arbitration.

Notwithstanding the above, there are certain basic situations over which Mexican courts will always have exclusive jurisdiction, including:

- Land and waters located within Mexican territory, including sub-surface, air space, territorial seas and continental platforms (rights in rem, rights arising from concessions to use, explore or exploit the same or leases thereon).
- Natural resources located in Mexico's exclusive economic zone.
- Actions of an internal nature by Mexican authorities, acting as such, and those of Mexican embassies and consulates abroad.

The decision to submit to foreign jurisdiction must also be "reasonable" and such choice should be made based on practical considerations, such as the domicile of the parties, the location of assets, applicable law, etc.

Arbitration

Practically any private dispute may be arbitrated in Mexico and, consistent with the foregoing, Mexican legislation has produced its own domestic rules, as well as adopted rules of an international nature.

The codes of civil procedures for each of the states, as well as the CC, contain provisions on arbitration as a means of settlement as do other laws with respect to banking, insurance, bonding and consumer protection. As examples of international rules, Mexico is a signatory to the following treaties:
- The New York Convention of 1958.
- The Panama Convention of 1975.

- The Uruguay Convention of 1979.

In January 1989 and in July 1993, the CC was amended in order to update its provisions on arbitration. Some of the relevant provisions are:
- Proceedings may be conducted in Spanish or in a foreign language and take place in the location chosen by the parties.
- The procedural rules may also be freely determined by the parties, including the applicability of those issued by an institution engaged in the resolution of disputes, such as the International Chamber of Commerce and the American Arbitration Association.
- The parties are also entitled to decide the applicable substantive law and if they do not address this question, the arbitrators must do so, considering the circumstances of the parties and their legal relationship.

Additionally, it is important to mention that arbitration awards are recognized in Mexico, regardless of the country in which they are issued and will be enforced in Mexico by Mexican courts unless:
- One of the parties did not have the legal capacity to submit to arbitration.
- The agreement to arbitrate was not valid.
- An interested party was not properly notified of the arbitration or of the appointment of the arbitrators or was otherwise not able to present its case.
- The appointment of arbitrators or other proceedings did not follow the rules approved

by the parties or in the absence of rules, the arbitration was not conducted in accordance with the applicable law of the jurisdiction in which the arbitration took place.

- The award refers to matters different from those contemplated in the arbitration agreement.
- The award is not yet obligatory or has been annulled or suspended by a court in the country where the arbitration took place.
- The Mexican court decides that the subject matter of the arbitration may not be arbitrated pursuant to Mexican law or its enforcement would violate public policy.

The Mexican Court System

The Mexican federal judicial system consists of the following courts:
(a) Federal Supreme Court of Justice
(b) Federal Elections Tribunal
(c) Collegiate Circuit Courts
(d) Unitary Circuit Courts
(e) District Courts

As required by the Federal Constitution, there are 11 Federal Supreme Court Justices, who hold office for a maximum period of 15 years. The Chief Justice is elected by the other justices every four years.

Finally, it is worth mentioning that a separate body, the Federal Judicial Council, is responsible for the administration, inspection and discipline of the

judicial branch, with the exception of the Federal
Supreme Court.

Chapter 45: Mexican Culture - Key Concepts and Values

Communication style

In Mexico, communication tends to be indirect and subtle, and presented in such as way as to be diplomatic and non-confrontational. Meaning is conveyed through nonverbal forms of communication or by less explicit verbal messages. Mexicans will often disguise "no" in responses such as "maybe" or "we'll see" with the aim of maintaining harmony and avoiding disappointing or offending the receiver.

When doing business in Mexico, it is vital to take this indirect approach with your Mexican counterparts as it will help to strengthen your business relationships.

Family

A fundamental Mexican value is that of the family and the place it holds in society. As a collectivist culture, the family unit is a dominating factor of daily life and the close ties between extended families and communities can have a major influence on individual behaviour. In a business context, the importance of family is evident in many Mexican companies.

Family-owned or controlled businesses are not uncommon and you will often find relatives working for the same company. These key families area also intrinsically connected to Mexico's political establishment and therefore establishing trustworthy contacts will be crucial for your success. This means that nepotism is a frequent occurrence in Mexican business culture and establishing trustworthy contacts will be crucial for your success.

Time

In Mexico, time is considered to be flexible, relaxed and circular, and is therefore unlimited. The word "mañana" is closely linked with the Mexican concept of time. In literal terms it means "morning" or "tomorrow", however it is also a way of saying "later". When hearing it in this context, you should expect things to be done some time in the near future, without great urgency or specific dateline in mind. Consequently, business meetings will run at a slower pace and your associates may take longer to reach a decision. Punctuality and time keeping are less closely observed; therefore, planning a tight daily schedule when doing business in Mexico should be avoided.

Chapter 46: Doing Business in Mexico (Pre-departure)

Working practices in Mexico

- It is important to schedule business appointments in advance and confirm them once you have arrived in Mexico.

- Business lunches are a favourable method of conducting business in Mexico, emphasising the more social aspect of Mexican business culture, and often go on for several hours. Breakfast meetings are also popular for getting to know your business associates, and to establish a more personal relationship.

- In most Mexican cities, working hours are generally 9.00 a.m. to 5.00 p.m., but may extend until 7.00 p.m. from Monday to Friday. Business is rarely conducted at the weekend, which is normally reserved for family.

Structure and hierarchy in Mexican companies

- The structure of Mexican companies is representative of the country's social structure. Hierarchy and social status are particularly significant in Mexican culture and the boundaries they create should be observed.

- Final decisions are generally made by a central authority figure. However, in Mexican business culture, general consensus is taken into account and subordinates are encouraged to openly express their point of view.

Working relationships in Mexico

- In Mexican business culture, cultivating close personal relationships and building trust are considered vital components for a successful working environment. Mexicans prefer to do business with people whom they know/trust and it is not uncommon to find many family members working for the same business.

- Respect is a key component in Mexican business culture and is reflected in the extensive use of professional titles and the formal "you" (usted). Mexicans place great emphasis on showing respect to others, especially to elder and more senior members of the group.

Business practices in Mexico

- Mexicans adopt a more formal approach to business relationships; therefore it is customary to address your Mexican business partner with the appropriate title. Courtesy titles such as "Mr" (Señor), "Mrs" (Señora), or "Miss" (Señorita), and professional titles (i.e. "Licenciado", "Doctor", "Profesor") should be used, followed by a surname. Since first names are generally only used with family and close friends, you should wait until invited to address someone in this way.

- During an initial business meeting, the most appropriate form of greeting is a warm and firm handshake. This should be done both upon arrival and departure and regardless of gender or seniority. When a more personal relationship has developed, it is not uncommon for business associates to kiss on the cheek or use a friendly embrace.

- An important part of Mexican business protocol is securing reliable contacts that can introduce and vouch for you. The use of personal introductions through a mutual friend or an appropriate professional is crucial for establishing trust and ensuring your future business success in Mexico.
- Business negotiations can be a lengthy process in Mexico and a certain element of bartering will be expected. It is also important to bear in mind that Mexican business people tend to base proposals and business decisions on the degree of personal trust established with the foreign counterpart and on some occasions on gut feelings.

Chapter 47: Conclusion

Your success in Mexico is therefore dependent upon your ability to establish, build and maintain good relationships.

Mexicans make friends first, then do business and you should be prepared to spend time socialising. Only move on to business when you have built up rapport. Face-to-face contact is crucial.

You need to invest time in developing relationships with people such as by going out to lunch (breakfasts are a good option if you want to avoid traffic in Mexico City), enquiring about their family and talking about your personal life. Sports (especially football) are a common interest between Mexicans, as well as British music which is very popular in Mexico, The Beatles are always a good talking point!

Fact File
- Official name – United Mexican States
- Population – 111, 211, 789
- Official Languages – Spanish, various Mayan, Nahuatl, and other regional indigenous languages
- Currency – Mexican peso (MXN)
- Capital city – Mexico City (Distrito Federal)
- GDP – purchasing power parity $1.559 trillion
- GDP Per Capita – purchasing power parity $14,200

Mexico is the site of advanced Amerindian civilisations and the northernmost and westernmost country in Latin America. Mexico's ethnic composition, its prominent regional identities and notoriously vivid culture, have all been shaped by the nation's history of immigration and various outside influences from the indigenous, (Toltec, Olmeca, Zapotec, Maya, Aztec, Huichol, Purapecha and Tarahumara).

Spanish and African civilisations:

The rich diversity of its many cultures is by far Mexico's most valuable asset. For those wanting to conduct business in this thriving environment, an understanding of this complex Mexican heritage and culture must be achieved in order to secure your future business success.

(Do's and Don'ts)

- DO translate all your marketing literature and any other documents for your business dealings into Spanish. Failure to do so may jeopardise your business potential.
- DO expect your Mexican business counterparts to converse at a much closer physical distance than you may be used to. A Mexican's sense of personal space is much smaller and physical contact is not frowned upon.
- DO take your time during business dealings with your Mexican colleagues and avoid pressing for final decisions, remember that

time in Mexico does not always equal money, as in some western countries.

- DON'T make direct and frequent eye contact when in conversation with you Mexican business associates. Mexicans tend not to make direct eye contact as a sign of respect.
- DON'T be overly aggressive while negotiating business deals, as it is considered rude.
- DON'T offer gifts of extremely high value. Gift giving is not a requirement of Mexican business etiquette, but a small gift will be gratefully accepted and appreciated.

Mexican Culture Quiz Time – True or False

1. During a business meeting, it is considered disrespectful to throw documents on the table.
2. If giving a gift of flowers, you should avoid the colour yellow. Yellow flowers are associated with funerals and symbolise death.
3. To give the "OK" gesture with the thumb and index finger in Mexico is considered vulgar.
4. Your business success in Mexico is primarily based on professional experience and know-how. Building and maintaining good personal relationships is considered less important.
5. Using the "psst-psst" sound to gain another's attention is considered rude and impolite in Mexican business culture.

Cultural Quiz - Answers
1. True.
2. True.
3. True.

4. False. Business relationships often take precedence over capability.
5. False. This is an accepted form of behaviour and not considered impolite.

Useful Spanish phrases
Hello Hola
Good day Buenos días
Good evening Buenas tardes
Good night Buenas noches
How are you? Cómo está?
Nice to meet you. Mucho gusto
Goodbye Adios
Please Por favor
Thank you Gracias
Sorry Lo siento
Excuse me Disculpe
How much is this? Cuánto es?
Too expensive Demasiado caro
Where is…? Dónde está…?
Toilets Baños
Ladies Señoras/Mujeres/Damas
Gents Señores/Hombres/Caballeros

Finally: Ten top Tips to Doing Business in Mexico

1. Research and plan early.
   • Is there a market there for you?
   • Is your competitive edge in the UK transferable to Mexico?
Desk research via the internet, suppliers, customers, trade associations, trade journal editors and exhibition organisers can be free of charge.

2. Seek out early sources of advice and expertise. This should save you time and money on wasteful activity and help to mitigate risk.

3. Get in touch with a global support network through UK Trade & Investment

4. Consider your pricing strategy. Pricing must be competitive – US dollar or Mexican peso pricing is the norm.

5. Think about language implications. Make the effort to produce brochures in Spanish – it makes a difference. Also think about translation of parts of your website.

6. Think about cultural implications. Make sure that your business cards are up to date and any titles included – Mexicans place a lot of importance on titles and good quality business cards.

Take business suits – Mexicans generally wear formal suits to all meetings. Try to visit Mexicans at their offices, rather than invite them to your hotel.

7. Think about your strategy. It is often beneficial to have a local partner or local presence. Think about your strategy; can your business model support margin reduction or transfer of intellectual property?

8. Arrange a programme of visits in the market. If you are new to business in Mexico, it is strongly advisable to arrange a programme of meetings through the local UK Trade & Investment office or other local contacts prior to travel.

In planning your itinerary, allow time at the end of your stay in Mexico to pay a second visit to those potential clients who have asked you to come back and see them again. Be prepared to socialise and do working lunches. Do not over-cram your time with meetings.

Allow plenty of time between meetings, as the larger cities can get very congested with traffic.

9. Take part in a guided market visit.

10. Follow up. Don't forget to follow up and don't let the contacts go cold.

Stay in touch with your Mexican contact/partner; don't let relationships drift, and make sure that you visit the market regularly.

Good Luck!

Made in the USA
Lexington, KY
14 January 2015